B1 Reading

Ten more practice tests for the **Cambridge B1 Preliminary**

Anna Phillips and Terry Phillips

PROSPERITY EDUCATION

© Prosperity Education Ltd. 2025

Registered offices: Sherlock Close, Cambridge
CB3 0HP, United Kingdom

First published 2025

Revised edition: 2026

ISBN: 978-1-915654-46-5

Original edition © Innova Content Ltd.

This publication is in copyright. Subject to statutory exception and to the provisions of relevant collective licensing agreements, no reproduction of any part may take place without the written permission of Prosperity Education.

This edition is published by arrangement with Innova Content Ltd.

INNOVATING LANGUAGE EDUCATION

The moral rights of the authors have been asserted.

'Cambridge B1 Preliminary' and 'PET' are brands belonging to The Chancellor, Masters and Scholars of the University of Cambridge and are not associated with Prosperity Education or its products.

Designed by ORP Cambridge

For further information and resources, visit:
www.prosperityeducation.net

To infinity and beyond.

Contents

Introduction	*v*
Test 1	*1*
Test 2	*13*
Test 3	*25*
Test 4	*37*
Test 5	*49*
Test 6	*61*
Test 7	*73*
Test 8	*85*
Test 9	*97*
Test 10	*109*
Answers	*121*

A digital platform for Cambridge exam preparation

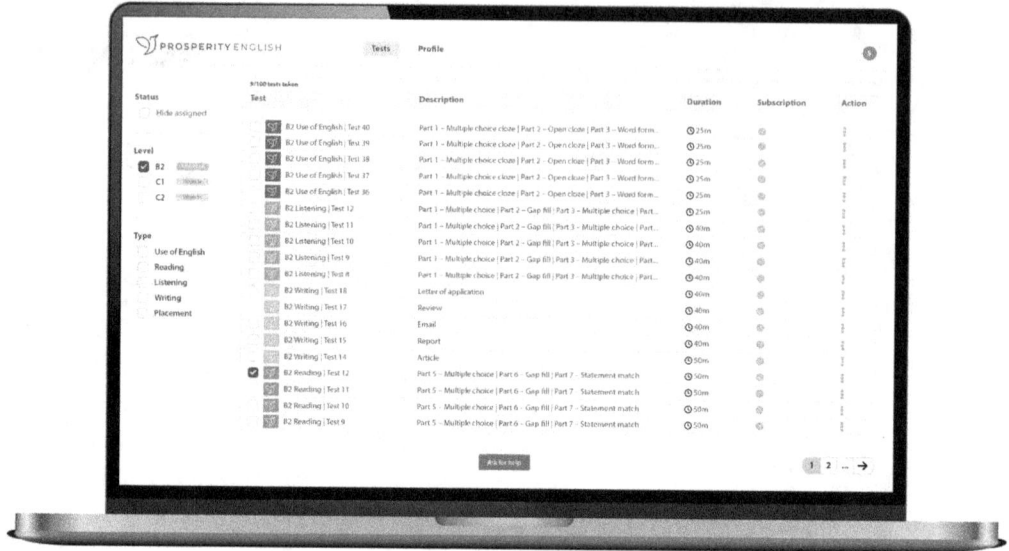

Prosperity English provides ample opportunities for repetitive practice, allowing you to reinforce your learning and improve your exam skills steadily.

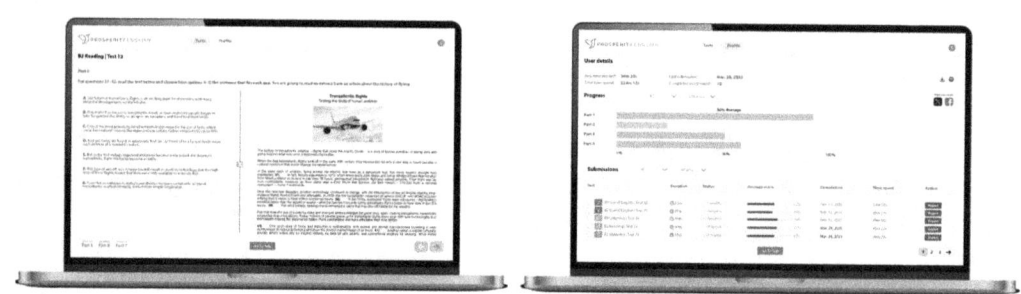

Try it for free

www.prosperityenglish.com

40% promotional discount code:
TIAB40

Introduction

Welcome to this edition of sample tests for the Cambridge B1 Preliminary Reading, which has been written to replicate the Cambridge exam experience and has undergone rigorous expert and peer review.

The B1 Preliminary English language exam is the third of six levels established in the Common European Framework of Reference (CEFR): A1–C2. Candidates of all ages can take the B1 Preliminary test. In the exam you will have 45 minutes to complete the Reading paper. This section has six parts, and is worth 25% of the final score.

The notices and texts should be similar to those found in real-world settings. Candidates must demonstrate their ability to understand and operate in such environments by choosing the correct answer. They will be asked to show command of vocabulary and grammar, as well as understanding of how a text is structured. Candidates must understand details, general meaning, as well as the writers' attitudes and opinions. At the end of the examination, candidates will be given five minutes to copy their answers into the write-in answer sheets.

	Number of questions	Number of marks	Task types	What do candidates have to do?
Part 1	5	5	3-option multiple choice	**Read five real-world notices**, messages and other short texts for the main message.
Part 2	5	5	Matching	**Match five descriptions** of people to eight short texts on a particular topic, showing detailed comprehension.
Part 3	5	5	4-option multiple choice	**Read a longer text** for detailed comprehension, gist, inference and global meaning, as well as writer's attitude and opinion.
Part 4	5	5	Gapped text	**Read a longer text** from which five sentences have been removed. Show understanding of how a coherent and well-structured text is formed.
Part 5	6	6	4-option multiple-choice cloze	**Read a shorter text** and choose the correct vocabulary items to complete gaps. An element of grammatical knowledge may be tested, e.g. complementation.
Part 6	6	6	Open cloze	**Read a shorter text** and complete six gaps using one word for each gap. Show knowledge of grammatical structures, phrasal verbs and fixed phrases.
Total	32	32		

For more information, visit the Cambridge Assessment English website.

This book contains 10 Reading tests (Parts 1–6), comprising a total of 320 individual assessments. You or your students, if you are a teacher, will hopefully enjoy the wide range of texts and benefit from the repetitive practice, something that is key to preparing for this part of the B1 Preliminary (PET) examination.

We hope that you will find this resource a useful study aid, and wish you all the best in preparing for the exam.

Cambridge B1 Preliminary

Reading

Test 1

© 2025 Prosperity Education.
'Cambridge B1 Preliminary' and 'PET' are brands belonging to The Chancellor, Masters and Scholars of the University of Cambridge and are not associated with Prosperity Education or its products.

Reading B1 | Ten more tests for the Cambridge Preliminary

Part 1

Questions 1 – 5

For each question, choose the correct answer.

1

Weston Discount Stores

No parking
Mon to Fri 8 a.m.–6 p.m.

NO loading or unloading

A You can park here on Sundays.

B You can't park here at any time during the week.

C You can stop here for a few minutes to pick up goods from the shop.

2

To: Jo
From: Helen

Let me know if you can still come over and help me with the project sometime over the weekend. If not, I'll ask Emily.

Helen

A Jo must confirm that she has asked Emily about the project.

B Helen needs to know if Jo and Emily can come to her house on Saturday.

C Jo needs to tell Helen if she is still able to help her.

3

Don't forget to give your name to Mr Lewis by the end of the week if you want to go on the school trip. Places are limited. It's first come, first served!

A Mr Lewis knows the names of the students who are going on the school trip.

B You must tell Mr Lewis this week if you are interested in going on the school trip.

C If you give your name to Mr Lewis this week, you can go on the school trip.

4

> Dear Students
> Please come to the school office to collect your test results on Wednesday 14th March from 11 a.m. until 4.00 p.m.
> You must bring photo ID.

A   Test results will only be given to students who take an identity card with a photograph.

B   Students with photo ID can get their test results any time on Wednesday 14th March.

C   Students can collect their photo IDs on Wednesday 14th March.

5

> Hi John
>
> Any thoughts about Saturday? I was going to suggest the new ice skating place, but it's not open until Monday.
>
> Mark

A   Mark wants John to go ice skating with him on Saturday.

B   Mark wants to know if John has visited the new ice skating place.

C   Mark wants a suggestion from John for something to do on Saturday.

Part 2

Questions 6 – 10

For each question, choose the correct answer.

The young people below all want to do an after-school club.
On the opposite page there are descriptions of eight clubs.
Decide which club would be the most suitable for the people below.

6  Ella is fifteen and loves maths and science, except physics. She wants to be a doctor and does a course in basic medicine on Friday evenings, so can't attend a club that day. ....

7  Ben is a good footballer, but he has a Saturday job so he isn't in the school team. He's interested in running, and quite good, but he wants to improve. He doesn't like jumping and throwing events. ....

8  Lily has two great loves – painting in oils and being on stage. She'd love to get better at both, but her parents say she can only go to one club because she has so much homework each evening. ....

9  Amy's father is an artist and her mother's a pilot. Amy is quite good at drawing and her father would like her to follow in his footsteps. But she's keen to learn more about flying. Amy goes to a dance class on Monday afternoons after school. ....

10  Tom is eleven and loves exercise of all kinds. He looks forward to gymnastics lessons at school and always takes part in the running and jumping events during sports day. ....

After-school clubs

A Art Club
Do you want to learn how to draw animals? Would you like to know the tricks in producing lifelike drawings of people? Or perhaps you love landscapes? At our club, you'll develop your skills with pencils and watercolours. [No oil painting because the oils are too expensive.] Mondays 4.00–5.00.

B Drama Club
Are you already an experienced actor? Or are you just starting out on your acting life? We meet in two groups, so there is something for everyone. Each week we look at a different part of performance, from controlling your voice to playing comedy and tragedy. Learn new skills while you are having fun. Tuesdays 4.00 to 5.00

C Maths Club
If you can't get enough maths in your lessons, come along and learn even more about the incredible world of numbers.
You'll find out about the history of maths and how it is used in everyday life.
Choose the club for your age group.
Age 11–12: Mondays 4.00–5.00
Age 13–14: Wednesdays 4.00–5.00
Age 15+: Fridays 4.00–5.00

D Science Club
The perfect club for anyone who wants to follow a career in science when they leave school. We meet in the physics lab, but we look at every area of science today, including new materials and the search for cures for illnesses and disease. Wednesdays: 4.00–5.00

E Gym Club
You don't have to be an expert gymnast to enjoy this club. Of course, if you are already good at jumping and swinging from ropes, you will get better. But even a beginner will have fun because we make every exercise into a game.
Open to all students from 10 up.
Thursdays 4.00 p.m.–5.00 p.m.

F The Cadet Force
Are you interested in the army, air force or navy? In our clubs, you can discover what it's really like to drive a tank, fly a plane or sail a ship. For ages 11–13, we have Army Club. At 14, you can stay in the Army Club or move to the Air Force or Navy.
Army: Mondays **Air Force**: Wednesdays
Navy: Friday
All clubs: 4.00 p.m.–5.00 p.m.

G Athletics Club
We meet on the sports field at 4.00 p.m. on a Tuesday if the weather is dry, or in the gym if not. We divide into groups who want to get better at running short, medium or long distances. Note: We don't include throwing or jumping events at this club.
Tuesdays 4.00–5.00

H Football Club
This club provides practice for students who are in the school teams. We teach you new skills and how to improve your existing skills. Come along at 4.00 on the correct day for your team.
Mondays: Under 12s
Tuesdays: Under 14s
Wednesdays: Under 16s
Thursdays: Under 18s

Turn over ▶

Part 3

Questions 11 – 15

For each question, choose the correct answer.

Bob Green (16) writes about … writing

I am sixteen years old, so people are often quite surprised when I tell them that I have already written three novels. I've even written a couple of plays, although I am not very proud of them. I started writing properly when I was nine years old. There was an illness at my school, which meant that we all had to stay at home for two weeks. I didn't get the illness, so for me it was just an unexpected holiday. I'd never enjoyed playing computer games or watching television, so I spent the first few days just reading. But then, one day I was reading something boring and I said to myself, 'I can do better than this.' So, I picked up a pencil and started to write. For my first piece of work, I filled up notebooks with handwriting until I got my first computer. Then I taught myself to type well. I do most of my writing now on the computer, although I do make a lot of notes in pencil when I'm working out the plot of a story.

My first writing effort was an autobiography. I had a few memories of my early life, like my first day at school, but I mostly relied on stories from my parents and my grandparents. For example, I asked them what happened on each of my birthdays. I didn't remember most of the events, but I put them into the autobiography. I had diaries from when I was six, but I couldn't use anything from them because it was all boring. I didn't put in any of our family stories because you had to know the people to find them funny.

I moved on from autobiography to novels. I've written a story set in the future with two female astronauts, and a historical novel set in the 17th century. My latest work is a modern crime story. The hero is not a police office, but she is really good at solving crimes. Of course, she works with a man who is not as clever as she is, so she has to explain everything to him. With an autobiography, you have a timeline, but with a novel, you must make sure that your readers don't get lost, so someone explaining things from time to time is good.

I say 'my readers', but the only person who has read my writing so far is my mother. She says my books are good and that I'm getting better. But soon I'll have to send my writing somewhere else and get a view from someone a bit more critical.

11 Bob started writing because

- **A** he was bored with having to stay at home.
- **B** he was confident about being more interesting.
- **C** he was ill and had to stay at home.
- **D** he didn't like computer games.

12 How does Bob create his writing now?

- **A** He types into a computer.
- **B** He writes in pencil in a notebook.
- **C** He writes in a notebook then types up his notes.
- **D** He plans the story then types.

13 What does Bob think is the most important thing with novels?

- **A** making sure that readers understand the timeline
- **B** having strong characters
- **C** his own memories
- **D** his parents and grandparents

14 What does Bob plan to do next?

- **A** Ask his mother to read all his work.
- **B** Work hard to make his writing better.
- **C** Get an opinion about his work from another person.
- **D** Have a look at someone else's writing.

15 What might Bob write in a covering email when he sends his latest novel for review?

A
I have been writing for seven years and have produced three novels, including this one, in addition to an autobiography.

B
I am an experienced writer of crime novels. My female hero solves crimes with the help of a male character.

C
Although I am quite young, I hope you will find this novel, which is set in the future, has an interesting plot and strong characters.

D
This is my third novel with the same main characters. You will see that the woman has to explain things, so the readers don't get lost.

Turn over ▶

Part 4

Questions 16 – 20

Five sentences have been removed from the text below.
For each question, choose the correct answer.
There are three extra sentences which you do not need to use.

Schools help the planet!
by Jill Brown, aged 13

We learnt this year in Geography that the planet is getting warmer. I think we all knew about the problem already. **16** ____ It is a huge problem and governments around the world are struggling to find answers. It seems that the problem is mainly caused by using too much energy. **17** ____ These gases go into the atmosphere. These are called 'greenhouse gases' because they hold heat in the same way that a greenhouse for growing plants is hotter than the garden which it is in. **18** ____ In the end, it will be impossible to live in many places because they will be too hot, or because the sea level will rise and cover islands, for example, in the Indian Ocean.

But our teacher said that this is not just a problem for governments. She said that we should not leave everything to other people. **19** ____ The teacher put us into groups to think of something we could do in our own school to save energy. My group decided that the school was too hot in winter. We suggested that the headteacher should tell the person who controls the central heating to turn down the boiler by one or two degrees. After we had presented our idea to the school, everyone agreed that it was a good idea. **20** ____

A	If we don't do something about this rise in temperature, the problem will get worse.
B	But now the teacher has given us actual facts and figures.
C	Plants often grow better in a greenhouse.
D	The headteacher asked for other suggestions.
E	The headteacher promised to do this.
F	We can all do something to help.
G	We use a lot of energy every day.
H	When we make electricity or burn oil in car engines, we produce gases.

Turn over ▶

Part 5

Questions 21 – 26

For each question, choose the correct answer.

Monkey see, monkey do

It is not clear where the word 'monkey' in English **(21)** .... from, but it could be from the word 'mannekin' in old Dutch, which means 'little man'. Monkeys are certainly man's closest **(22)** .... They are amazing creatures. Some types of monkey can understand written numbers, and a few can even count, add up and multiply.

Monkeys can learn sign language and **(23)** .... simple ideas to humans. A monkey called Washoe had a vocabulary at the end of her training of thirty-four signs. She could link signs together to make new sentences, for example, 'Open the fridge' or 'Please come quickly'.

Monkey parents, **(24)** .... human parents, teach their young useful life skills. For instance, during research in the 1940s, scientists gave their monkeys sweet potatoes as part of their diet. Some of the monkeys didn't like the taste of the dirt on the outside, so they took the potatoes to the **(25)** .... to wash them. The parents taught their young this **(26)** .... and now, eighty years later, monkeys from that group still wash their food.

21	A comes	B arrives	C gets	D reaches
22	A family	B relatives	C parents	D relationships
23	A communicate	B talk	C speak	D say
24	A including	B as	C like	D similar
25	A edge	B seashore	C mountains	D sand
26	A behaviour	B way	C condition	D thought

Part 6

Questions 27 – 32

For each question, write the correct answer.
Write **one** word for each gap.

Sports Day
by Ellen White

Last week the school sports day **(27)** .... held at the Town Sports Club. As always, it was a great success! The weather was beautiful, and I think that all the spectators and the competitors **(28)** .... a good time. I certainly did!

Over two hundred students from every year at the school took **(29)** .... in more than 50 events. **(30)** .... were running races for every distance up to 1,000 metres, plus jumping and throwing events. The students competed in four teams, which each had a colour – Blue, Yellow, Green and Red.

After a very close contest, the Green team came first, narrowly beating the Red team into second place. **(31)** .... this is the third year in a row that the Green team has won, the headteacher decided to give a special cup to their team captain **(32)** .... they can keep in their display cabinet for ever.

Cambridge B1 Preliminary

Reading

Test 2

© 2025 Prosperity Education.
'Cambridge B1 Preliminary' and 'PET' are brands belonging to The Chancellor, Masters and Scholars of the University of Cambridge and are not associated with Prosperity Education or its products.

Part 1

Questions 1 – 5

For each question, choose the correct answer.

1

A This shop is open at lunchtime on Saturday.

B This shop closes at lunchtime on weekdays.

C This shop is only open for three hours at the weekend.

2

Trip to Windsor Castle

Meeting today in Room C4 at 1.00 for anyone interested in going on this trip next week.
Ms Green
[If you have given me your name already, you don't need to come.]

A You must go to C4 at 1.00 if you want to go on the trip.

B The meeting is for people who might want to go on the trip and haven't booked.

C Students who are already booked on the trip must go to C4 at 1.00.

3

New Message
To: John
From: Alan

Hi!
What are you planning to do for the science project? I know we can't work together, but could you suggest something for me?
Alan

A Alan wants an idea for the science project.

B Alan needs some help from John with finishing the science project.

C Alan is asking John to help him write his science project.

4

Dear Student,

Exams for Year 12 will be held in the school hall during the week beginning 15th June. To reduce noise, rooms A1–A6 will not be used that week. Ask your teacher where you will be working.

A   Students normally in A1 to A6 do not have lessons during week beginning 15th June.

B   If you are usually in a class in rooms A1 to A6, you will be in a different room for one week.

C   You must be quiet if you are studying in rooms A1 to A6 because of exams in the hall.

5

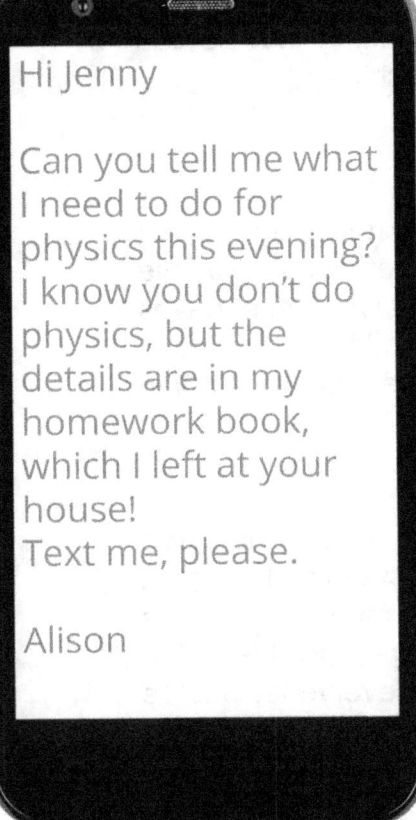

Hi Jenny

Can you tell me what I need to do for physics this evening? I know you don't do physics, but the details are in my homework book, which I left at your house!
Text me, please.

Alison

A   Alison needs Jenny to help her with the physics homework for this evening.

B   Alison wants Jenny to tell her what they must do for physics homework.

C   Alison needs to get her homework book to do her physics homework.

Turn over ▶

Part 2

Questions 6 – 10

For each question, choose the correct answer.

The young people below all want to buy a computer app for the summer holidays.
On the opposite page there are descriptions of eight apps.
Decide which app would be the most suitable for the people below.

6 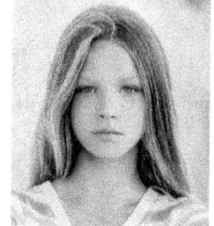 Sophie is fourteen. She is going over 1,000 kilometres by car with her parents to their holiday hotel, and she needs something for the journey there and back. She sometimes struggles with reading, and she prefers games of some sort which she can play on her own.

7  Luke is twelve. He has a summer job in a different town. He is going to cycle because the bus is too expensive, but he wants something that he can listen to on the long journey each day.

8  Emily is fifteen. She plays the guitar and sings. She plays in a band in her hometown. She'd love to earn her living as a musician when she leaves school. During the summer holidays, the band can't meet and play because the others are going away. Emily will be bored.

9  Alya is 16 and lives with her father and three younger sisters. She loves cycling. However, she doesn't have a bike at the moment because she has grown too tall. She is responsible in the summer for making meals for everyone, but it's difficult to make quick meals which everyone likes.

10  Oliver loves football and is in the school team. He gets bored in the summer holiday because he lives a long way from his friends, who are football mad. He bought a book of puzzles last summer, but he wasn't very good at them. Oliver wants to study biology when he goes to university.

Computer apps for the holidays

A **Number 1!**
Over 5,000 fantastic rock, pop and dance tunes. You can:
- mix
- add instruments
- create special effects
- record your own voice
- add videos

When you have finished, send it to studio. Maybe you will get a recording contract!

B **Great stories from around the world**
Listen to all those stories which you have heard about but never been able to understand or finish!
- Charles Dickens
- Tolstoy
- Jane Austen
- Edgar Allan Poe

and hundreds more!
Each story is available at three age levels, so you can choose the right version for you: 10–12, 13–15 or 16+
Control the audio from your smartphone or Bluetooth headset.

C **A History of the World – in maps**
History's boring, right? Just kings, queens and dates? Wrong!
History is the fascinating story of where we came from and how we got here. And the best way to see it is with maps of key moments. How big was the Roman Empire in the first century? Where did Marco Polo go in the 13th century?

D JOURNEY TO THE CENTRE OF YOU
This fantastic app takes you through the human body inside a tiny camera.
- Visit your lungs and find out how you breathe.
- Explore your heart and travel in your blood to the ends of your fingers!

Have fun in your stomach when your food arrives!

E **Puzzler**
Do you love puzzles? Then this app is for you.
There are hundreds of word puzzles, number puzzles and picture puzzles like 'Name the logo'.
Play on your own or with friends.
You can even create your own puzzles and amaze your friends.

F **Cycle Mapper**
Do you spend a lot of time cycling for pleasure … but want new places to explore? Our app plans interesting routes in your area. You choose what you want to see – the countryside, small villages, the coast. Then choose the distance and the difficulty (lots of hills or nice, flat country).
For smartphones only.

G **Fast Food Maker**
Fast food is great, isn't it? But it's not very healthy and you can't make it in your own home. Well, you couldn't … until now!
We offer over 500 recipes for healthy meals which you can make in 5 or 10 minutes.

H **Football Boss**
How do you enjoy your favourite game when there's no football on the television in the summer? Here's how! You – and up to 3 friends – are in charge of a top football club like Manchester United or Bayern Munich, or another from over 200 top clubs. Decide how you want your team to play, buy and sell players, and play against your friends. For 2 to 4 players.

Turn over ▶

Part 3

Questions 11 – 15

For each question, choose the correct answer.

Do you ever miss a deadline?

15-year-old Jackie Black has some advice!

Most of my schoolwork involves some sort of deadline (the date it must be finished by). Sometimes they are very short, and the teacher wants homework returned the next morning. In other cases, the deadline is a week or a month away, like projects, or even three months away, like exams. With long deadlines, you must keep people informed about your progress if you are having problems. Never wait until the last minute to say to the teacher, 'Sorry, Miss. I haven't started yet.' And never say, 'I'll hand it in next Monday,' when you know it will be impossible.

In most cases, a piece of work has a deadline when it is given to you. The teacher says, 'I need this by Wednesday,' or 'Make sure you hand it in before 10th December.' If a deadline isn't given, don't think, 'Oh, good. I can do this in my own time.' And don't get the deadline from another student. Maybe they got it wrong. Some people don't bother to check the deadline, then a few weeks later, they suddenly realise the work is due in the next day.

One good thing about deadlines is that you don't have to hand in every piece of work at the same time. But to benefit from that, you must put all your work in order. Plan what you must do first, next and last. Add when each piece of work is due to your phone calendar. For long deadlines, make sure you are reminded one month, one week, two days and one day before. Some work is more important than others, so put that in red in your calendar.

Another key point is that a piece of work is very rarely one thing, for example, a single exercise. Maybe you have to do Exercises 1–4 on page 50 for maths this evening. Unless the teacher has told you that, say, Exercise 4 is the most important, you should divide the time available by four. So, if you can spend one hour on maths, give yourself 15 minutes on each exercise. Explain to the teacher the next day if you couldn't finish one of the exercises in the time given. For a long piece of work, like a project, divide it into sections.

11 Jackie thinks it's important to

    A   tell people how you are getting on with work.
    B   apologise if work is late.
    C   say why you haven't handed in a project.
    D   tell people when you will finish a project.

12 What should you do if the person doesn't give you a deadline?

    A   Do the work as quickly as possible.
    B   Do the work in your own time.
    C   Ask the person if there's a deadline.
    D   Get the deadline from another student.

13 What is one of the benefits of deadlines?

    A   Deadlines are easy to add to phone calendars.
    B   They mean you don't have to plan your work.
    C   Work can be handed in at different times.
    D   You have more time to complete the work.

14 How should you deal with each piece of work?

    A   Divide the work by four.
    B   Find out what is the most important part.
    C   Find out the amount of work involved.
    D   Divide the work by the time available.

15 A teacher has just asked Jackie to read a novel. How will she organise the task?

A
1 Ask which section is most important.
2 Check the deadline with another student.
3 Put the deadline in her phone calendar.
4 Set the phone to remind her.
5 Do the important work first

B
1 Ask for the deadline.
2 Work out the amount of time.
3 Divide the work into sections.
4 Put each section into her phone calendar.
5 Start the work.

C
1 Ask for the deadline.
2 Check the amount of work.
3 Work out the amount of time.
4 Divide work by time.
5 Put each section into her phone calendar.
6 Do the work.

D
1 Ask for the deadline.
2 Check the amount of work.
3 Work out the amount of time.
4 Divide work by time.
5 Put each section into her phone calendar.
6 Set the phone to remind her many times.

Turn over ▶

Part 4

Questions 16 – 20

Five sentences have been removed from the text below.
For each question, choose the correct answer.
There are three extra sentences which you do not need to use.

The bottle that went round the world
by Josh Gillway, aged 14

What is the most famous object in the world? Is it a building, like the Colosseum in Rome? Or a painting, such as the *Mona Lisa*? Perhaps it's a plane, like a jumbo jet. **16** According to a recent online survey, it is a bottle which is more than 100 years old. It seems that people recognise it in most countries in the world.

The survey checked the most famous logo in the world, too, and it belongs to the same company that produces the bottle. **17** Perhaps the logo is the most famous because it has not changed in over 130 years, unlike the logos of other companies which have been around that long. **18**

The story of the drink is older than the bottle and the logo. In 1886, a man called John Pemberton, who had a chemist's shop, invented a new type of drink, using the leaves of the coca plant, sugar, kola nuts and a few secret ingredients. **19** Then, he sold the recipe to another chemist, Asa Candler. Candler mixed the drink with soda. At first, Candler sold it in his chemist's shop, then he began selling the syrup to other drugstores. After a short time, two businessmen got a licence from Candler to sell the drink in bottles. It appeared in many different-shaped bottles until 1916. **20**

A	Actually, the most famous object is a car.
B	He sold it as a medicine, but the drink was not particularly successful.
C	In fact, it's none of these things.
D	In that year, the famous bottle was produced and has stayed in production ever since.
E	It is even older than the bottle, because the bottle first appeared in 1888.
F	Which company produces the bottle?
G	The bottle and the logo are, of course, from Coca-Cola.
H	The things are still secret.

Part 5

Questions 21 – 26

For each question, choose the correct answer.

Digital pets

Do you have a pet? Parents sometimes buy a pet for a child **(21)** .... they keep asking for one, without thinking about the problems that pets involve. All pets need feeding, and you need to **(22)** .... a dog for regular walks, or it will become fat and unhealthy.

If you don't have a pet already, perhaps you should start with a digital pet before you ask your parents to buy a real pet, **(23)** .... a dog, a cat, a fish or even a snake. Digital pets live on your smartphone or your computer. You have to give them food every day and **(24)** .... them to do what you say. If you forget to feed them, they die. If you don't teach them to **(25)** .... to your orders, they may run away. If you can't look **(26)** .... a digital pet, then it might be difficult for you to deal with a real one!

21	A	because	B	so	C	when	D	although
22	A	give	B	bring	C	take	D	have
23	A	as	B	like	C	such	D	example
24	A	learn	B	talk	C	explain	D	teach
25	A	listen	B	hear	C	know	D	get
26	A	for	B	after	C	from	D	with

Part 6

Questions 27 – 32

For each question, write the correct answer.
Write **one** word for each gap.

Are you a great photographer?

Do you take photographs of everything you see? **(27)** .... you do, perhaps you should enter the school photography exhibition. You can choose anything to photograph, from the birds in your garden **(28)** .... the clouds before a storm. You can enter one photograph each in any of the five groups – People, Animals, Plants, Buildings and Weather. We **(29)** .... looking for photographs which are funny, strange or amazing. Last year, one person won the Animals group with a photo of their dog wearing glasses, and the Weather group **(30)** .... won by a photo of clouds in the shape of a face.

Send in your photographs by 1st November to the email address below, with your personal details. We need to know your name, your age and the school **(31)** .... you are attending. We **(32)** .... announce the names of the winners on 17th November.

Cambridge B1 Preliminary

Reading

Test 3

Part 1

Questions 1 – 5

For each question, choose the correct answer.

1

A   Only people with permission can park here in the evenings.

B   You cannot park here at 10 if you have a permit.

C   Permit holders can park here at any time.

2

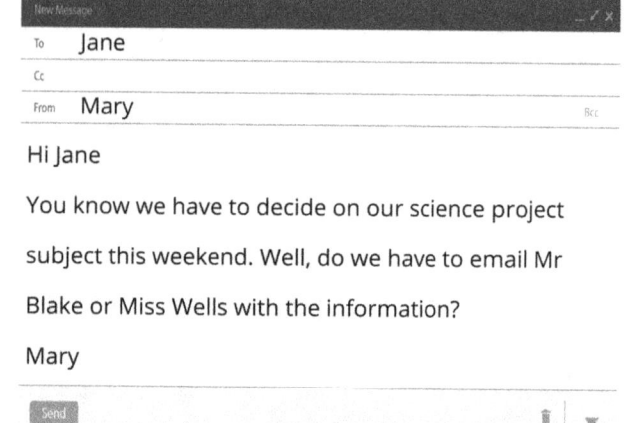

Hi Jane

You know we have to decide on our science project subject this weekend. Well, do we have to email Mr Blake or Miss Wells with the information?

Mary

A   Mary needs Jane to confirm which teacher to inform about her science project.

B   Mary wants to know what subject Jane has chosen for her science project.

C   Mary wants to know when to send information about her project to the teacher.

3

After-school clubs

Please sign up for after-school clubs this week. Years 1 to 4 should attend three clubs, but Years 5 and 6 cannot attend more than two.

A   If you are in Year 4, you can only go to two clubs.

B   No students can go to more than three clubs.

C   Year 5 students can go to three clubs.

4

Hi Jo

Do you want to come to the meeting about the school play tomorrow? It's no problem that you haven't acted before. There are lots of parts, including some with no speaking. But I think you would be good as the mother. It's up to the drama teacher.

Zara

A   Jo can be in the school play if she doesn't want a speaking part.

B   Jo can't take a speaking part because she hasn't acted before.

C   The drama teacher could pick Jo for a speaking or a non-speaking part.

5

Dear Parents

School closes at 1.00 p.m. on 15th July instead of 3.45. Please make arrangements to collect your child/children early. If you are not able to collect them, please send me a letter explaining how your child/children will get home that day.

Mrs Symes
Headteacher

A   All parents must send a letter if they are collecting their child on 15th July.

B   If parents can collect their child/children on 15th July, they needn't send a letter.

C   If a child can't go home with a parent, they can go home at the normal time.

Turn over ▶

Part 2

Questions 6 – 10

For each question, choose the correct answer.

The young people below all want to go on a day trip with their parents next weekend. On the opposite page there are descriptions of eight day trips in their local area. Decide which trip would be the most suitable for the people below.

6  Joe is 11 and he loves anything to do with water. He enjoys swimming and all kinds of water sports. He also likes anything adventurous, like climbing mountains or going deep under the ground.

7  Emma's parents take her somewhere every weekend. They usually visit a large garden, and Emma is often bored. But this weekend they have said that she can choose a trip, and she wants to go somewhere historical.

8  Dan loves history and wants to visit a castle or old building. He's studying the 1500s at school at the moment, so would like to go somewhere which was built then. The only problem is that his mother can't climb very well.

9  Ellen's hobby is drawing. She particularly likes doing animals, and last month her parents took her to a zoo, thinking she would love it. But she didn't like the way the animals were treated.

10  Carl is 15. He likes going on boats on rivers or lakes, or on the sea. He likes playing around in water, too. He doesn't mind how high a ride is at a water park, but he doesn't like being in small places.

Day trips from Cornford

A Blue Caves
These amazing spaces were made over millions of years by the Blue River running under the Kingland Hills. Enjoy a fascinating tour by boat through the caves, ending with a light and music show in the largest of the caves, the Great Hall. It glows blue from the strange rocks on the walls.
Open Weekdays 2.00 p.m.–6.00 p.m.
Weekends 10.00 a.m.–4.00 p.m.

B Turnbury Village
Would you like to see how people lived in the countryside a hundred years ago? The village of Turnbury has not changed since then, because everyone living there left the village following a terrible flood, which damaged many of the houses. Nobody has lived in the village since then. But now you can visit Turnbury one day a week, where a guide will tell you all about life there a century ago.
Mondays 9.00 a.m.–4.00 p.m.

C Roseland Animal Gardens
Do you like seeing wild animals but hate the idea of them being locked in small cages?
At Roseland, all our tigers, lions, elephants and giraffes, and many more animals, are free to move around the natural landscape at a safe distance from visitors.
And the monkeys sit and watch you when you're eating at our outdoor café!
Every day 10.00 a.m.–sunset

D Waterworld
If you like water sports, this is the place for you! You can water ski on our huge lake or go over The Waterfall in a rubber boat. If you are very brave, go down The Gorge, riding the waves at high speed.
Only suitable for children 12 or older.
Weekdays 10.00 a.m.–5.00 p.m.
Sat and Sun 11.00 a.m.–4.00 p.m.

E River Cruise
Sail slowly down the wide Blue River from Kingland to Weston. On the way, pass through many beautiful villages and go past the old castle at Appleby. Then stop for lunch or tea at Shilton.
Round trip: 3 hours
Saturday and Sunday only
Departures at 10.00, 12.00 and 2.00 p.m.

F Appleby Castle
Built in 1100, this castle is a perfect example of Norman architecture, with tall, thin windows and many arches. Much of the original building has survived, so Appleby is popular with history lovers.
You must book a guided tour before you arrive.
Note: There are a lot of steps, so this is not suitable for wheelchair users or people who find steps difficult.
Open daily: 10.00 to 5.00

G Weston House and Gardens
The house dates from the time of Henry VIII (1491–1547). The beautiful gardens were first laid out in the 17th century and are a good example of garden design of that time. The gardens are perfect in spring and summer, and the house is full of interest all the year round.

H Cycle Tours
Do you want to explore the Kingland Hills or the coast around Weston, but you don't have a suitable bike? Hire one from us! We give you a helmet for the day and a range of routes, from easy to challenging.
We have a limited supply of bikes, so you must book in advance.

Turn over ▶

Part 3

Questions 11 – 15

For each question, choose the correct answer.

There's no *I* in 'team'!

15-year-old Matthew Jones writes about his hobby, football.

I can't remember when I fell in love with football, but I was very young. My mother loved the sport, and she was in a local team. I loved seeing her play and score! In fact, there is a story in our family that I shouted 'Goal!' from my pram when she scored once. According to the story, I was about a year old at the time.

Even before I went to school at five, I was quite good at kicking a ball. Every time I went to the park or to the beach with my parents, we started kicking around a football, and my mother worked on my technique. I remember her kicking balls high in the air and shouting, 'Watch the bounce!' all the time. Children often can't predict how a football will bounce, so the ball goes over their heads.

There was a football team at my primary school, and I was good enough to be chosen. We had practice games every Friday afternoon and proper games every Saturday morning. By the age of 10, I was quite an experienced player. My favourite position was striker. I could run very fast, so my teammates kicked lots of long balls over the defence and I ran onto them, judging the bounce correctly and often scoring a goal.

When I went to secondary school, I didn't think I would have any problem getting into the school team – and I didn't. I was chosen after the first practice. But after three or four games, the sports teacher, Mr Willis, said he was not happy with the way I was playing. It's true that we lost all those games, but I already had about five goals to my name, so I was shocked. Then he asked me, 'What is your most important job in this team?' I replied immediately. 'Scoring goals, Sir.' But Mr Willis shook his head. 'No, it's helping the team to win.' 'Yes, Sir,' I said. 'By scoring goals.' He shook his head again. 'By making sure that goals are scored,' he said. It seems that I didn't pass the ball enough, but always took a shot at goal, even when another player was in a better position to score. That's when I learnt that there's no 'I' in 'team'!

11 Matthew

    A   remembers seeing his mother score a goal when he was in his pram.
    B   fell in love with football when he was about one year old.
    C   went to see his mother playing football as a young child.
    D   knows exactly when he first began to love football.

12   How did Matthew's mother improve his football technique?

    A   She taught him to judge a bouncing ball.
    B   She kicked the ball high in the air.
    C   She played football with him on the beach.
    D   She shouted at him a lot when he was playing.

13   Why was Matthew successful in football at primary school?

    A   He had practice games and proper games every week.
    B   He could run fast and score a lot of goals.
    C   The other people in his team knew how to help him to score.
    D   He played as a striker.

14   What did Matthew learn from Mr Willis about playing football?

    A   Each person in a team has a different job.
    B   The job of a striker is to score goals.
    C   A striker should pass the ball a lot.
    D   Each person in a team must help the team to win.

15   What did Mr Willis write about Matthew after the most recent football match?

A	B
Matthew is good at watching the bounce of the ball. That is why he is such a good goalkeeper.	Matthew doesn't score as many goals as he used to. He must learn to watch the bounce of the ball more carefully.

C	D
Matthew used to try to score every time he got the ball. Now he is much more of a team player. He didn't score in this game, but he made two goals.	Matthew needs to be more selfish when he gets in front of goal. He had two opportunities to score in this game, but he passed the ball instead.

Turn over ▶

Part 4

Questions 16 – 20

Five sentences have been removed from the text below.
For each question, choose the correct answer.
There are three extra sentences which you do not need to use.

How to complain
by Jade Mills, aged 13

Do you complain when something goes wrong with a product or a service, like the delivery of something you've ordered online? Most people don't complain, but in many cases, complaints are successful if they are done in the correct way.

I'm not going to talk about complaining in a shop or a restaurant. **16** Even if the shop assistant or the restaurant manager knows that the complaint is correct, it is very unlikely that they will take you seriously. But we all buy a lot of things online now, and in most cases, you do not have to talk to someone to make a complaint. **17**

Before you start to complain, decide what you want to happen as a result of your complaint. Do you want to exchange the item? **18** If the company offers vouchers instead, are you prepared to accept them? When you contact the company, be polite, even if you feel angry. Secondly, be clear. **19** Have notes on the date you placed the order, when it was received, what exactly is wrong, and so on.

If you get involved in live chat, find out who you are talking to. **20** You might need to go back to it if the company does not deal with your complaint quickly. I don't complain a lot like this, but, when I do, I nearly always get what I want.

A	I don't think you should complain in shops and restaurants.
B	I think it is very difficult for a child or a teenager to make a complaint face to face.
C	Or do you want to go to speak to a manager?
D	If possible, take a screen shot of the chat and print it, with the date and time.
E	It is usually done by email or, more and more, by taking part in a live chat.
F	You have to write a letter and post it to the company.
G	Or would you prefer a refund?
H	Write down all the facts before you contact the company.

Turn over ▶

Part 5

Questions 21 – 26

For each question, choose the correct answer.

How does the world work?

How did the world work before electricity? For thousands of years, people used the natural power of water to run simple machines. These machines could make flour from wheat, for example, and do jobs **(21)** .... cutting wood or beating metal into shape.

In the 18th century, people started to heat water in boilers and use the power of steam to run machines. Steam power was **(22)** .... more powerful than running water or falling water, and it led to the rise of the railways in many countries, as well as steamships which could **(23)** .... oceans quickly.

In the late 19th century, water was used to make electricity for the first time. In the north of England, a scientist **(24)** .... to bring electricity into a house in 1878. Edison invented the electric lightbulb in 1880, and by 1881 the streets of the town next to Niagara Falls were lit by electricity from the water **(25)** .... of the Falls.

Now, the world works by electricity, and most electricity is made from **(26)** .... coal, oil or gas. But making electricity in this way is the main cause of global warming. Perhaps we will have to go back to making electricity from water in the future.

21	A such	B includes	C like	D as
22	A many	B much	C lot	D very
23	A sail	B go	C travel	D cross
24	A able	B could	C managed	D invented
25	A power	B speed	C energy	D weight
26	A lighting	B burning	C firing	D heating

Part 6

Questions 27 – 32

For each question, write the correct answer.
Write **one** word for each gap.

Summer Camp
By Sophie Bell

Do you get bored in the long summer holidays? Do you miss meeting and playing (27) .... your friends? Do you want to do something different and exciting this summer?

At *Summer Camps 4 You* we offer a range of different experiences in the mornings.

- At Mountain Camp, you learn to ski and snowboard, or you improve your skills in these sports.

- At River Camp, (28) .... is a whole range of water sports, including water skiing and canoeing. You can also learn river fishing

- At Beach Camp, we have surfing and windsurfing, as (29) .... as swimming. You can also learn sea fishing

In the afternoons at all three camps, you have fun with your new friends in a whole variety of games and activities. You can choose (30) .... to do, from learning to draw and paint, to (31) .... a new sport or learning a new musical instrument.

In the evenings, we usually have a barbecue or, (32) .... the weather is cold or wet, we eat in one of the beautiful restaurants on our site.

Cambridge B1 Preliminary

Reading

Test 4

© 2025 Prosperity Education.
'Cambridge B1 Preliminary' and 'PET' are brands belonging to The Chancellor, Masters and Scholars of the University of Cambridge and are not associated with Prosperity Education or its products.

Part 1

Questions 1 – 5

For each question, choose the correct answer.

1

End of Summer Sale!

Starts 1st September for 14 days

All clothes 50% off except children's coats and jackets

- A You can buy everything at half-price here on 7th September.
- B Children's clothes are not all included in the sale.
- C The sale ends on 21st September.

2

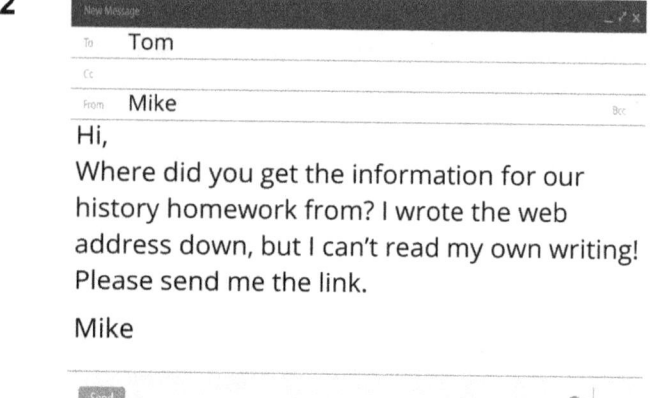

To: Tom
From: Mike

Hi,
Where did you get the information for our history homework from? I wrote the web address down, but I can't read my own writing! Please send me the link.

Mike

- A Mike wants a website address from Tom.
- B Mike needs to know some information for their history homework.
- C Mike is asking if Tom knows a good place to go for information for their homework.

3

School Office

Mon–Fri: 8.00–5.00
Sat and Sun: Closed
Call 067 892 345 during office hours.
At any other time, call 068 845 734 and leave a message.
We will return your call as soon as possible.

- A When the office is closed, you cannot speak directly to a person.
- B You should only call 068 845 734 at the weekend.
- C If you phone on Sunday morning, somebody will call you back before 5.00.

4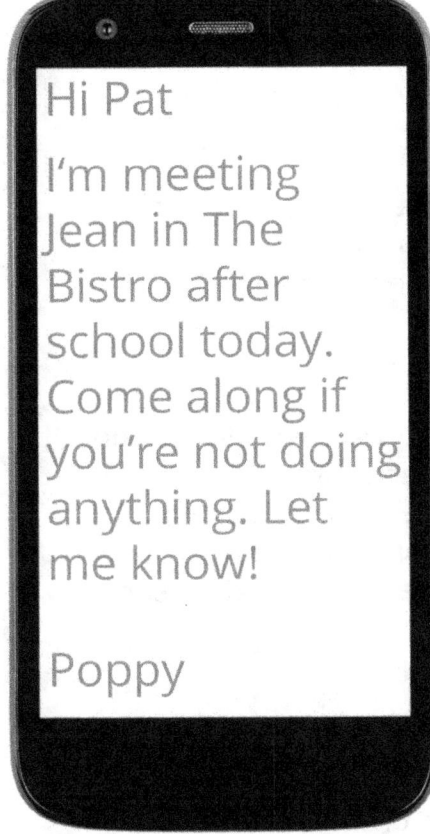

A Poppy wants to know what Pat is doing after school.

B Poppy wants Pat to meet Jean after school.

C Poppy would like Pat to join her and Jean at The Bistro.

5 Dear Parents

Several children have been sent home today with a temperature. Please keep your child at home if their temperature is higher than normal, but phone the office before 9.00 to confirm that your child won't attend that day.

Mr Barnes
Headteacher

A The headteacher wants to know if a child is ill.

B Parents must call the school if they are not sending their child.

C All parents should keep their children at home this week.

Turn over ▶

Part 2

Questions 6 – 10

For each question, choose the correct answer.

The young people below all want to buy a birthday present for a brother or sister.
On the opposite page there are descriptions of eight products.
Decide which product would be the most suitable for the people below.

6  Rob's little brother Jimmy is six. He loves stories and reads all the time. Rob's parents are going to buy Jimmy some new clothes, but Rob knows Jimmy will be a bit disappointed if he doesn't have anything new to read. Rob needs a clever idea for a good present.

7  Alice's youngest sister is eight. She says she wants to be a doctor for animals when she grows up, and her bedroom is full of drawings of snakes and parrots. She is very popular at school, and she often spends Saturday night at a friend's house.

8  Alex's brother is 11. His parents have just bought him a bicycle because he is starting a new school and will have to ride there every day. He has told Alex he isn't looking forward to it because he will get bored.

9  Eve's sister May is 12. She and Eve share a bathroom, but Eve can never get in there. 'Why don't you just have a quick shower?' she often says to her sister. But May says she prefers baths – long, hot ones, while she listens to her favourite music station. Eve wants to buy May something which makes having a shower fun.

10  Owen's brother Harry is nine. He has just got his first handheld computer and spends all his time playing on it. Owen says it's much more fun actually 'being' an astronaut and flying to the moon, for example, than just reading about it in a book. Or 'in a boring book', as Harry always says.

The perfect gift company

A Bath Book Rest
Do you love long baths … and do you also love reading? Why not do them both at the same time, with our super bath book rest? It fits on any size of bath and supports both small and large books.

B Fish Radio
If you want to listen to your favourite radio stations while you are having a shower, you need the Fish Radio. You take it into the shower with you. You needn't worry about the water getting inside, because it can't!

C Sleep Sheep
It can sometimes be difficult to get to sleep. At least, it used to be before we invented the *Sleep Sheep*. This lovely warm toy sleeps in bed with you. Press its nose and its eyes light up. Pull its ears and *Sleep Sheep* says, 'Close your eyes and go to sleep.' Then it sings a song. You can choose your favourite song from 20 options.

D Travel Bed
Do you go to sleepovers in your friends' houses? If you do, you need Travel Bed. It's like a sleeping bag, but it comes in a number of designs. There's a dog, a cat, a horse, a lion, a tiger, and many more pets and wild animals. The Travel Bed has its own pillow.

E BookSpeaker
If you cycle or walk to school, it sometimes gets boring. This is where *BookSpeaker* comes in. Just download your favourite stories from the *BookSpeaker* website and listen to them on the *BookSpeaker* Bluetooth headphones while you are cycling or walking.

F Adventure!
There are 30 different adventures in this fantastic computer game. You can be a pirate looking for buried treasure, an explorer trying to find a lost city, a diver looking for an ancient ship at the bottom of the sea, and lots more. Choose who you want to be and what you want to search for … and off you go!

G Bookworm
Do you eat your way through books at speed? With Bookworm, that isn't a problem. As soon as you finish one book, download a new one from the Bookworm site and carry on reading. We have both fiction and information books, and there's something for every age group.

H The Complete Bicycle Question
Question: What does a child need once they have a bicycle?
Answer: *The Complete Bicycle Book.* Find out how to repair a tyre, fix a chain, raise and lower the seat and the handlebars, and how to keep your bicycle shining and in great condition.

Turn over ▶

Part 3

Questions 11 – 15

For each question, choose the correct answer.

An actor's life for me – maybe!

16-year-old Ethan Morris writes about being an actor.

I've been shy for as long as I can remember. It's probably because we moved so many times when I was young, and I had to try to make new friends every time. I hated it. Even as a young child, I didn't know what to say when I met people. It always came out wrong. I used to go home afterwards and go over a conversation again and again in my head. I went red just remembering.

One day, when I was about 15, my older brother said, 'Why don't you come along to the youth theatre with me?' I thought he was joking. I couldn't imagine anything worse. I remembered drama classes at school and the annual school play, when I couldn't remember my lines and I just stood on stage being a tree or a frog and looking stupid. But he said the group wasn't like that and they didn't do plays. Each week, they act out scenes from real life, like a conversation at a bus stop with a stranger, or in a doctor's waiting room. These acting exercises help them learn about real-life communication.

Somehow, I was brave enough to go. I think I saw it as my last chance. And my brother was right. It wasn't embarrassing, perhaps because the leader of the group, Layla, was so good. Slowly, from the acting exercises, I began to learn how to communicate with new people, even girls of my own age.

I'm still shy. That's the funny thing. I still don't really want to meet new people, but I have a solution. When I meet someone new, I become an actor. I play the part of me meeting someone new. If I say something silly or trip over and hit my knee, it's OK because it isn't me. It's me playing the role of me!

I'm not sure if my solution is a good thing or not. I explained it to Layla, and she thinks it's fine. It certainly helps me get through lots of new situations. I don't want to be a professional actor, but I have a feeling that I might be an actor for the rest of my life, in a way.

11 Ethan thinks he's shy because

    A   he moved many times when he was young.
    B   he had to keep trying to make new friends.
    C   he met a lot of people as a young child.
    D   he often said silly things to people.

12 Why didn't Ethan want to go to the youth theatre group?

    A   because he didn't want to be in the school play
    B   because he thought it was a joke
    C   because he thought it would be like drama classes
    D   because his brother was in it

13 What did Layla want the children to learn?

    A   how to be things like trees and frogs
    B   how to talk to strangers
    C   how to remember lines for the school play
    D   how people communicate in real life

14 What did Ethan learn from the youth theatre?

    A   to be a different person with new people
    B   to enjoy meeting people
    C   not to say silly things
    D   not to be shy

15 What did Layla say to the school drama teacher about Ethan recently?

A

> Ethan is still very shy. I'm not sure that he has learnt much from his time with the youth theatre.

B

> When Ethan came to his first meeting, he was very shy. But he joined in with everything, and now he is a different person.

C

> Ethan has learnt to deal with the world in a particular way, but I don't think it is the right way.

D

> Ethan should stop playing different people in his everyday life and just be himself.

Turn over ▶

Part 4

Questions 16 – 20

Five sentences have been removed from the text below.
For each question, choose the correct answer.
There are three extra sentences which you do not need to use.

A difficult decision
by Alice Mills, aged 14

My older sister, Jess, had to make a decision last year. She is seventeen now, so last year she had to decide whether to stay on at school for two more years. [16]   But Jess didn't really want to do this, because she has never liked school much. She hated maths and wasn't interested in science. She couldn't see the point of studying a foreign language, because she didn't intend to go and live in another country.

The one subject which she liked at school was music, because she is a brilliant musician. [17]   She also writes really great songs. I even like some of them, and I'm her sister! Jess plays in a rock band, and last year the band was beginning to get money for playing in concerts. The other people in the band had left school, so they were doing two or three shows a week. [18]   Should she leave school and join them full time?

In the end, Jess made her decision just before the end of the school year. To help her decide, she made a list. [19]   The main advantage was that she would be following her dream. She would also not have to study maths and science subjects anymore. She put the bad things on the other side, like making our parents unhappy. [20]

Jess finally decided, and she is happy with her decision. What do you think she did?

A	But Jess could only do some of the shows because of her schoolwork.
B	One person in the band had a part-time job.
C	Our parents really wanted her to stay on.
D	She can play the guitar and the piano, and she's a good singer, too.
E	Our parents are normally quite happy people.
F	She put the good things about leaving school on one side.
G	She wasn't any good at art and hated PE.
H	The main worry was that the band might fail.

Part 5

Questions 21 – 26

For each question, choose the correct answer.

Wright … or wrong?

Most people have heard that the Wright Brothers were the first people to fly a plane with an engine. But were they really the first?

Alberto Santos-Dumont was born in 1873 in Brazil, South America. But in 1891, Alberto's father sold his farm and **(21)** .... the family to France. In Paris, the teenage Alberto went up in hot air balloons, which were very **(22)** .... at the time. Then, in 1898, he built his own balloon, which he called *The Brasil* after his home country. In **(23)** .... , Alberto designed several airships – balloons with engines and controls, so the pilot can change **(24)** ....

In 1901, Alberto flew around the Eiffel Tower in one of his airships. It was a great **(25)** .... He became one of the most famous people in the world at that time. In 1906, Alberto flew 60 metres just above the ground in his own plane. From that moment, some newspapers started to call him 'the father of flying'. However, people slowly began to hear about the Wright Brothers, who flew for 12 seconds over a **(26)** .... of 36 metres, three years earlier.

21	A	carried	B	moved	C	travelled	D	located
22	A	used	B	many	C	popular	D	known
23	A	also	B	well	C	too	D	addition
24	A	direction	B	way	C	route	D	road
25	A	travel	B	winning	C	achievement	D	flying
26	A	length	B	distance	C	line	D	way

Part 6

Questions 27 – 32

For each question, write the correct answer.
Write **one** word for each gap.

Building a playground
by Jack Lewis

I go to a school in the middle of a lot of new houses. The area is very pleasant, **(27)** .... until last month, there was nowhere for young children to play. My friends and I decided to **(28)** .... something about it.

We talked to our headteacher and she thought **(29)** .... was a great idea. She even made a call to the head of the local government, Mr Peters. He said that **(30)** .... we could prove there was a demand for the playground, he would use some of the money which he had for the parks in the town.

My friends and I asked all the people in the area **(31)** .... had young children to sign a letter to Mr Peters. We managed to get 1,215 signatures, and three months ago we took the letter to the government offices.

Mr Peters called our headteacher the next week to say that he was happy that the case for the playground **(32)** .... proved. Within two weeks, workers started to build the playground, and we opened it with Mr Peters at the beginning of last month.

Cambridge B1 Preliminary

Reading

Test 5

© 2025 Prosperity Education.
'Cambridge B1 Preliminary' and 'PET' are brands belonging to The Chancellor, Masters and Scholars of the University of Cambridge and are not associated with Prosperity Education or its products.

Reading B1 | Ten more tests for the Cambridge Preliminary

Part 1

Questions 1 – 5

For each question, choose the correct answer.

1

School Uniform

We have the uniform for all local schools in our shop NOW except King Edward's [available from Monday]

A   You can get your school uniform here today, unless you go to King Edward's.

B   This shop does not sell the uniform for King Edward's.

C   You can get the King Edward's uniform here until Monday.

2

To: Chris
From: Dave

Hi Chris,
How are you getting on with the science homework? I think the answer to Exercise 2 is 4, but I've also made it 5. Help!
Dave.

A   Dave can't do Exercise 5 and needs Chris to help him.

B   Dave wants Chris to confirm the correct answer to Exercise 2.

C   Dave is asking Chris whether they have to do Exercise 2, 4 or 5.

3

Food!

You are not allowed to eat food from home in the classrooms. If you bring sandwiches, take them to the restaurant at lunchtime.

A   This notice is for students who have school lunch in the restaurant.

B   The school does not allow students to bring food from home.

C   You must not have your sandwich lunch in a classroom.

4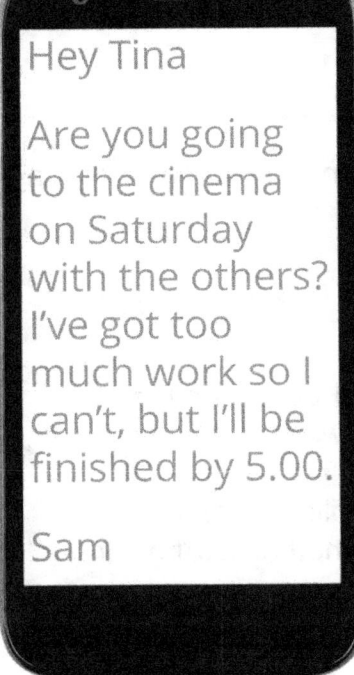

A   Sam is going to do schoolwork on Saturday evening.

B   Sam can meet Tina after 5.00 on Saturday.

C   Sam is going to the cinema with Tina and the others.

5   Dear Parents

The School Fair is on Saturday 4th May. If you are making food, such as cakes or pies, please send it in with your child on Friday. I'm afraid we can't accept anything before then.

Ms Collins
Headteacher

A   The headteacher wants to know which parents are making food.

B   Parents must send in food sometime this week.

C   Friday is the only day that children can take in food for the fair.

Turn over ▶

Part 2

Questions 6 – 10

For each question, choose the correct answer.

The young people below all need to earn some money during the summer holidays in July and August.
On the opposite page there are descriptions of eight jobs.
Decide which job would be the most suitable for the people below.

6  Joe is 12. He loves history and geography, and he knows his local area very well. His parents call him 'the early bird' because he gets up early every day, even in the school holidays, and goes out cycling. He doesn't care whether it's hot or cold, raining or sunny.

7  Nina is 16. She is going away with her parents in August. She wants to earn some money in July for the holiday. She doesn't mind what she does, even cleaning!

8  Mike is 14. He really looks forward to the summer holidays because he hates getting up at 7.00 to go to school. He's a very good artist and can also play the violin. He is happy to take care of his younger brother and sister – but not first thing in the morning.

9  Olivia is 16. She's in a rock band in her free time, where she plays the guitar and piano. She loves rock music, but concerts are so expensive that she can't usually afford to attend even the ones in her own area.

10  Grace is a very responsible person. She is only 13, but she looks after the house for her father, who is often away on business. She loves animals and plants and is quite a good gardener.

Summer jobs for kids!

A Film Extras for Star Movies
We are in your area during the summer. We need young people aged between 12 and 15 for some crowd scenes which we are filming in the town centre in July. You do not need to be an experienced actor. You don't even have to learn lines. We pay you £20 a day just for you to be yourself. At least 5 days' work.

B Finding the Past
Did you know that Romans lived in your town over 2,000 years ago? We are now digging in the Green Park area and we need volunteers to help us. It can be boring to slowly move the earth away from a possible Roman belt or necklace ... until the moment when you uncover it, and give it to one of the experts for cleaning and dating. No money, but great pleasure. July and August.

C Summer Camp Activity Leaders
We are holding a summer camp for children aged 8 to 12 at King Edward's School for 6 weeks in July and August. We pay £50 a week for boys or girls aged 14 to 17 to look after our children during afternoon activities. We pay £100 per week if you have a special skill, like playing a musical instrument, which you can teach the children.

D
Cornford Garage is opening a hand car wash and cleaning service for the summer to help with cleaning all those dirty cars inside and out before they go off for their touring holidays. We give you special clothes, so you don't get your own clothes wet or dirty. You get £10 an hour and you can work for up to 20 hours per week. You must be 15 or over.

E Car Wash Workers
We need volunteers to go through all the things which kind people bring into our shop in Roman Way. Don't worry! You don't have to sell anything. Your job is to organise things into male and female clothes, stories and information books, and so on.

F Charity Shop Helpers
Some of our regular delivery girls and boys go on holiday in the summer, so we need some temporary help. You must be over 11 and willing to get up early so that newspapers are delivered to everyone on your round by 8.00 a.m. at the latest. We pay £15 per week for 1.5 hours work per day.

G Newspaper Delivery
Do you want to be a cleaner?
You probably don't want to be a cleaner when you leave school, but we will have hundreds of applications for our cleaning jobs. Why? Because you clean up at the Cornford Rock Concert on July 23rd to 25th – and you have free tickets to ALL the stages between your cleaning jobs! Plus, we pay £50 a day. Apply now if you are over 15!

H House Sitting
We are looking for children over 12. Many people in our town go on holiday for two or three weeks in the summer and want someone to look after their house, their garden and their pets while they are away. You don't have to live in the house, but you must go to each house once a day to feed animals, water plants and take in any deliveries. £10 per week for each house you look after.

Turn over ▶

Part 3

Questions 11 – 15

For each question, choose the correct answer.

What is 'home'?

16-year-old Lucy Hall writes about home.

When I was born, my parents were living nearly five thousand miles from their home countr , the UK, in a very hot place called Oman. They owned a language school there, and they were so busy that they didn't go back to their own country very often. In fact, I think I was about two before I even visited the place which they called 'home'. Clearly, they loved it, but to me it was just like Oman, but colder.

While we were all living in Oman, my parents had to work long hours at the school, so they couldn't look after me a lot of the time. Occasionally, I went with them to the school, but it was boring, so I preferred to stay at home. I had a babysitter called Virgie, who was lovely, and I don't remember ever being unhappy as a child. When my parents came home, we had fun, but when they weren't there, I had fun with the babysitter instead.

Virgie came from a place where rice was the main food, so I learnt to eat rice from an early age. I still love rice to this day – plain, white rice, with nothing else. When I finally came to live in my home country, as my parents call it, children of my age thought I was strange. They loved potatoes, especially chips, but for me, rice was the best.

When I was four, my parents decided that they had to return home so that I could start school there. I could see that they were excited. I had to say goodbye to some friends, but the move wasn't terrible for me because Virgie was allowed to come, too. She stayed for a while, but she obviously missed Oman. My parents didn't have to work such long hours, so they could look after me more.

I have now lived in the UK since I came here at four. My parents have taken me back to Oman several times on holiday. Sometimes they say, when we arrive in the UK or even Oman, 'Do you feel you're coming home?' But people are more important to me than places.

11 How did Lucy feel about her parents' home country at first?

    A It felt like home.
    B It didn't feel like home.
    C It felt the same as Oman.
    D She loved it.

12 While she lived in Oman,

    A Lucy spent a lot of time with her babysitter.
    B Lucy often went to her parents' company.
    C Lucy missed her parents during the day.
    D Lucy looked forward to her parents coming home.

13 Why does Lucy like rice so much?

    A Her parents cooked rice for her when she was young.
    B Virgie often gave her rice.
    C She doesn't like chips.
    D She likes the plain white colour.

14 Why wasn't Lucy too unhappy about leaving Oman?

    A She was excited about going home.
    B She didn't have any friends at nursery school.
    C She didn't have to say goodbye to Virgie.
    D She would be with her parents more.

15 Lucy's teacher asked her class to answer the question: What is home? What did Lucy write?

A
It's the place where you were born. That is more important than family or friends.

B
Home is where your mother or your father is. If you are not with your parents, you cannot feel at home.

C
Home isn't a country or a town. If you are with people you love, you are home.

D
I have lived in two countries, so I don't really have a home.

Turn over ▶

Part 4

Questions 16 – 20

Five sentences have been removed from the text below.
For each question, choose the correct answer.
There are three extra sentences which you do not need to use.

How to talk to people
by Liz West, aged 15

Conversation should be easy. You ask someone a question, they answer, and everything flows from there. But many people, especially teenagers, find it difficult to start a conversation with a new person. So here are some ideas for conversation starters that should work in almost every situation.

You can say something nice about a person or something they own. **16** ____ The other person will usually say thank you and tell you where they bought it, or even how much it cost. You can ask more questions if it seems to be interesting.

Another conversation starter is to ask a question about the person's background. Be careful, because you don't want to sound rude. **17** ____ Once again, the conversation might continue well from there.

Questions about the future are also a good way in. You can ask a question like 'What would you like to do after you leave school?' or 'Do you want to start your own company?' **18** ____ Sometimes they even want to talk about their fears for the future. Someone might say, 'I don't intend to stay in this town.' Then you can start to discuss the good and bad things about the place. Questions with 'if' work well, too. **19** ____

Whatever you do, try not to ask something which allows the other person to give a short answer, like, 'Yes', 'No' or 'Fine'. **20** ____ 'What was the best thing about school last week?' will have much better results.

A	For example, a question like 'How's school?' is hopeless.
B	But questions like 'Have you lived here long?' should be fine.
C	For example, 'How old are you?'
D	You can start with 'That dress looks terrible.'
E	For example, 'How would you feel if your parents wanted to move to another country?'
F	For example, 'That's a lovely T-shirt!' or 'I really like your jacket.'
G	You could say, 'How are you?'
H	People usually like to talk about their personal hopes or plans.

Part 5

Questions 21 – 26

For each question, choose the correct answer.

Water, water, everywhere!

There is an enormous amount of water on Earth. In fact, water covers about 71% of the Earth's surface. So, why do about 10% of the world's population not have access **(21)** .... fresh water? And why don't we have **(22)** .... water to water crops and give to farm animals?

The reason is because only 3% of the world's water is fresh water, in rivers and lakes. The **(23)** .... 97% is found in the seas and oceans and is salt water. As everyone knows, salt water cannot **(24)** .... used for drinking or watering crops. It is possible to take the salt out of seawater. However, it is expensive to do, and many countries which don't have much rainfall are **(25)** .... poor to build the necessary factories.

Some fresh water is locked in ice that floats on salt water in the Arctic and Antarctic. Why does ice float? Because water is the only liquid which takes up more **(26)** .... as it gets colder. Other liquids, like milk, take up less space as they get colder. But water gets bigger, so ice is lighter than liquid water.

21	A	of	B	to	C	from	D	for
22	A	enough	B	more	C	some	D	any
23	A	rest	B	final	C	total	D	other
24	A	are	B	be	C	is	D	have
25	A	too	B	very	C	so	D	much
26	A	area	B	size	C	space	D	place

Part 6

Questions 27 – 32

For each question, write the correct answer.

Are you a great artist?

Do you love drawing and painting? **(27)** .... you do, this competition is for you. There are prizes in three groups. You can choose **(28)** .... drawing with pencils, painting with watercolours, or painting with oils. Within each group, there are three age ranges: 7–10, 11–14, and 15+.

We are looking for works of art **(29)** .... show good technique but are also original. Whether you prefer your subjects **(30)** .... be people, animals or landscapes, we want to see your work. But please make it your own. Do not copy a photograph or painting from another person.

You don't **(31)** .... to send us your actual work. All we need is a high-quality photograph. Send it to the email address below by 21st March with your personal details. The winners **(32)** .... be announced on 13th April.

Cambridge B1 Preliminary

Reading

Test 6

Part 1

Questions 1 – 5

For each question, choose the correct answer.

1

> Due to illness, this shop will be closed until further notice. All enquiries next door.

A You can't buy anything from the shop at the moment.

B You can buy items from the shop next door.

C The shop will stay closed permanently.

2

> To: Students registered for badminton club
> From: Fred
>
> Please transfer your fees for the badminton club by 9 p.m. Monday at the latest or you will lose your place.
> Thanks
> Fred

A This is the last chance for students to register for the club.

B There are very few places left for the badminton club.

C Students who don't pay on time will not be able to play badminton at the club.

3

> **Student exchange programme**
>
> If interested in taking part with students from the UK, please sign below.
>
> **Note:** All students in Years 7 to 12 may apply; exam students in Year 13 cannot apply.

A You must have signed permission to take part in the exchange programme.

B Students from Year 10 are allowed to go on the exchange.

C The exchange trip is only for students over the age of 13.

4 Careers Advice Centre

Interviews every day this week except Monday – during lunch break.

Remember to bring your CV with you.

No appointment needed – just drop in!

A It is essential to have an appointment before you can have a career interview.

B Students need to take their CV to the advice centre on Monday.

C Students can go for an interview at any time during their lunch breaks Tuesday to Friday.

5

Hi Adam

Working late today. Could you get some food or order a takeaway? Happy to eat anything – you choose!

Grace

A Grace wants Adam to organise dinner.

B Grace wants Adam to cook dinner.

C Grace wants Adam to suggest a meal for dinner.

Turn over

Part 2

Questions 6 – 10

For each question, choose the correct answer.

The young people below all want to watch a TV programme.
On the opposite page there are descriptions of eight TV programmes.
Decide which programme would be the most suitable for the people below.

6  Emily is 13. She enjoys reading detective stories and also loves animals and wildlife. At the weekend she watches films with her family, so she can only watch other TV programmes during the week.   ....

7  Ed is 16 years old. He is a bright student and enjoys watching serious, intelligent programmes. He doesn't like reality TV or sitcoms. He can only watch TV at the weekends, because he has too much homework during the week.   ....

8  Bella is eight. She loves animals and she'd love to be a vet when she grows up. She enjoys watching game shows and anything funny. She can't watch anything after 8 p.m. because that's her bedtime.   ....

9  Sam is 14. He is a fan of police and detective drama programmes and is crazy about sport. He thinks most cartoons are silly. Sam doesn't get home from school until 6 p.m., and then he has dinner. So the earliest he can watch TV is 7 p.m.   ....

10  Ava is 11 and enjoys comedies and cartoons. She also enjoys watching game shows, because she loves fun challenges and quizzes. She has music lessons after school on Tuesdays and Fridays, so she doesn't have time to watch TV on those evenings.   ....

TV programmes

A Star Kids
The auditions are over and it's time for the annual final of *Star Kids*! This year's competition has 12 amazing finalists, aged from 6 to16. They include Maria, the little girl with the BIG voice! And Joe with his delightful dog, Trix.
Who do you think the winner will be?
Don't forget to download the app and vote for your favourite act.
Friday 8.00 p.m.

B Green Planet
A journey around the world looking at the incredible variety of wildlife and nature in over 60 countries. This amazing documentary took four years to film. You can expect the latest technology and effects. Green Planet uncovers the wonderful hidden world of animal and plant life and the environmental challenges they face in the 21st century.
Sunday 7.30 p.m..

C Happy House
A children's game show hosted by Lily Best. Each week there are two teams of one boy and one girl. They represent schools from around the country. There are three fun rounds: Make a Mess, Mini Moto Grand Prix and Happy House Quiz. The winning team gets a great prize
Tuesday 8.00 p.m.

D Sherlock Holmes and the twins
A family story about mystery and crimes in Victorian London. It features the famous Arthur Conan Doyle detective, Sherlock Holmes, and the 12-year-old twins, Michael and Martha, who live next door at No 223 Baker Street. In this week's episode, the twins help Sherlock find his missing friend, Dr Watson.
Thursday 6.00 p.m.

E Chalk and cheese
Crystal and Charlie may be sister and brother, but they are completely different from each other, like chalk and cheese! In this comedy, Crystal is top of the class, but Charlie is the class joker. This week Crystal is organising a school debate, but Charlie has other plans …
Thursday 8.00 p.m.

F Newspaper delivery
A news programme for young people who want to know more about current issues and stories affecting our world. It features interviews with celebrities, international topics and the latest on environmental situations. Competition for Young Reporter of the Year: send us your news videos!
Monday 8.00 p.m.

G Junior Sport
Follow the latest sporting news, meet the top stars from around the world and look ahead to the weekend's events. This week's show features top-class table tennis stars. You need great speed and strategy skills to win at this sport.
Wednesday 7.30 p.m.

H Dangerbear
An entertaining cartoon series for younger children.
Our hero is Dangerbear and her young assistant Monty, the mouse.
Follow the pair around the world and in space on their adventures in their dangercar.
Saturday 8.00 a.m.

Turn over ▶

Part 3

Questions 11 – 15

For each question, choose the correct answer.

Creative Solutions

16-year-old Luisa Long writes about her hobby, inventions.

My mum is a scientist and my dad's an engineer. My dad is always taking things apart and putting them back together again. Once it was a complete car engine! My brother and I enjoyed helping him, and we learned a lot that way.

During one of our school holidays, when I was about 10, my brother and I got really bored, so Mum gave us a fun challenge. She asked us to think of ideas for an invention and draw a picture of it. I had the idea of a pair of trainers that used kinetic energy to charge your phone while you were walking. When I think about the idea now, I can see the technical problems, but it gave me the passion for inventing!

A year or so later, I entered a national competition for kids' inventions. My invention was a power flower that generates electricity from solar power – that's power from the sun. The 'leaves' and 'petals' on the flower are made from solar panels, with wires that travel down to a generator in the flowerpot. The great thing is that the flower looks attractive – in fact, it's a piece of modern art. It looks much better than all those ugly solar panels in fields

The thing I like most about inventing things is that you need both technical skills and creative ones. You need to start by identifying a need or a problem, and then thinking of ideas for a solution. Your solution must be practical, of course, and you need different skills to design the solution. Experience is important too, because that tells you what things will or won't work. It also helps to be enthusiastic and optimistic, and you need to be very organised.

Not all of my ideas work, and the first time I got negative comments it was a setback. But I decided to learn from the experience. One of my teachers said, 'Start small and then make it good.' I think that's excellent advice, don't you?

11 Luisa probably became an inventor because

   A   she wanted to please her parents.
   B   she liked taking cars to pieces.
   C   she helped her father with his projects.
   D   she learned a lot from her brother.

12 What does Luisa feel now about her first invention?

   A   It inspired her to become an inventor.
   B   It wasn't a very good idea.
   C   She thought it was a brilliant idea.
   D   You can get kinetic energy from a pair of trainers.

13 Why is the 'power flower' a useful invention?

   A   It's a beautiful design.
   B   It makes electricity from sunlight.
   C   It has a generator and solar panels.
   D   It replaces unattractive solar panels.

14 What does Luisa say about being an inventor?

   A   People will say unhelpful things if your idea doesn't work.
   B   You can't be an inventor if you don't have the right skills.
   C   Having determination is more important than having experience.
   D   Inventions are about finding a solution to a problem.

15 What might a science magazine journalist write about Luisa now?

A
Luisa needs to believe in her own abilities and stop depending on other people for her ideas.

B
Luisa has really improved as an inventor. Her ideas are practical and things that people really need.

C
Luisa does not like it when people make negative comments about her inventions, so she must learn to be less sensitive.

D
Luisa could be a great inventor, but she needs to find a tutor who can improve her skills in technology.

Turn over ▶

Part 4

Questions 16 – 20

Five sentences have been removed from the text below.
For each question, choose the correct answer.
There are three extra sentences which you do not need to use.

Volunteering in a hospital
by Maisy Ross, aged 14

Last winter my grandmother was sick and had to stay in hospital for a while. [16] One of the nurses showed me how to help my grandmother to sit up and how to hold a special drinking cup for her.

One day I saw a notice in the hospital asking for volunteers. [17] However, I read the information carefully and realised the minimum age was 14. I'd had my 14th birthday a few days earlier!

When I got home, I went online and got more information about hospital volunteering. As well as helping with patients on the wards, there were other things you could do. For example, you could be a hospital guide. This means you greet patients and visitors to the hospital at the main door. [18] Some hospitals are huge, and people are often stressed or worried when they arrive, so this is an important job.

At first, I couldn't decide which voluntary job to do. [19] On my ward, which is for elderly female patients, I visit in the evenings. My first job is helping to serve dinner and to encourage patients to eat a little. [20] They really enjoy that!

Volunteering has been a great experience, and I'm studying hard at school so I can be a nurse or even a doctor!

A	After that, I sometimes do puzzles with them or we just talk.
B	However, in the end I became a ward visitor.
C	In hospital, the patients have their breakfast very early.
D	I visited her several times a week to help her with food and drinks.
E	I thought perhaps they only wanted adults.
F	Nurses are sometimes on duty for 12 hours.
G	Then you accompany them to the correct part of the hospital.
H	Visiting hours at the hospital are from 5.00 p.m. to 7.00 p.m.

Part 5

Questions 21 – 26

For each question, choose the correct answer.

Power walking

Would you enjoy walking more if your **(21)** .... charged your mobile phone? A company in the UK has **(22)** .... a pavement which turns movement into electricity. It is the latest alternative power source that helps us rely less on fuels such as oil and gas. These pavements use the energy from people's steps to power street lights nearby and USB charging **(23)** .... Each footstep can produce about five watts of green electricity, which means about 25 footsteps can charge a mobile phone.

More than 35 countries in the world, **(24)** .... Hong Kong, India, the USA and Korea, are now using these special pavements. In London, pedestrian footsteps power Bird Street and **(25)** .... birdsong during the day and street lighting when it gets dark.

In future, tiles used to make the pavements will replace **(26)** .... floor tiles. They could be installed in offices, schools, shops and other public places. It's a really bright idea!

21	A moves	B steps	C walks	D stops
22	A developed	B thought	C used	D improved
23	A situations	B plugs	C positions	D points
24	A containing	B involving	C including	D with
25	A provide	B deliver	C support	D prepare
26	A for	B frequent	C fixed	D regular

Part 6

Questions 27 – 32

For each question, write the correct answer.
Write **one** word for each gap.

Visit to waterpark
by Jodie Miller

Do you enjoy swimming and water activities? Would you like **(27)** .... exciting day out with your classmates? Then you will love this year's school trip to World of Water.

At World of Water there's a huge range **(28)** .... activities:

- There are 30 different rides and activities to enjoy. **(29)** .... you like speed and excitement, there are several really fast rides. The longest ride is Stormcatcher, which is great fun!

- You can also enjoy activities and races with your friends. And if you need to relax for a while **(30)** .... all that excitement, there are pools for that too.

- There are two main areas, inside and outdoors. But, of course, in bad **(31)** .... like rain or strong wind, the outside area will be closed.

Included in the price of your ticket is a meal in the Waterside Café. All students on the trip will wear wristbands that you can **(32)** .... for lockers, rides and food.

Cambridge B1 Preliminary

Reading

Test 7

Part 1

Questions 1 – 5

For each question, choose the correct answer.

1.
The Big Sale
Online sale starts on Thursday!
30–40% off everything* plus FREE delivery and returns.
Hurry! Offer ends at midnight on Monday.

*Offer does not apply to goods that already have a discount.

- A You can only order items on Friday to get a discount.
- B You can get a discount on most items over the weekend.
- C You need to hurry if you want to return items.

2.
To: Jade
From: Sara

Hi Jade!
Can you remind me what the deadline is for our environment project?
And is it 3,000 words or 5,000? I wrote the details in my notebook, but I lent it to Fred and now he's off sick!
Thanks
Sara

- A Sara wants Jade to help her with the project.
- B Sara is asking Jade if she knows Fred is sick.
- C Sara needs information because she hasn't got her notes with her.

3.
Attention all drivers on the school campus!

Please note there is a

10 mph speed limit

for all vehicles, including bicycles and motorbikes.

- A No vehicles are allowed to travel at over 10mph.
- B The speed limit only applies to cars.
- C Cars are not allowed on the school campus.

4

Dear Parents,

You are invited to attend our annual careers fair. Many representatives will be there with information about what they can offer students when they leave school.

Visit our website for more information or to book an appointment with a representative.

A Parents have to email the school to make an appointment with a representative.

B The school holds an event to help students choose careers every year.

C Parents must visit the website if they want to attend the fair.

5

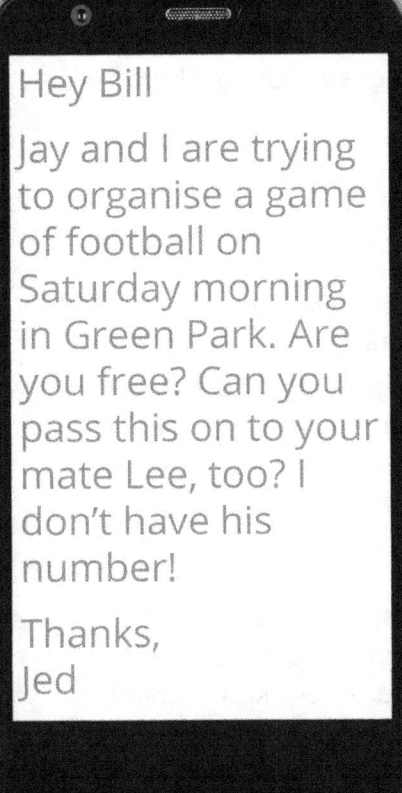

Hey Bill

Jay and I are trying to organise a game of football on Saturday morning in Green Park. Are you free? Can you pass this on to your mate Lee, too? I don't have his number!

Thanks,
Jed

A Jed wants to meet Bill's friend, Lee.

B Jed wants to know what Bill is doing on Saturday morning.

C Jed would like Bill to join the football team in the park.

Turn over ▶

Part 2

Questions 6 – 10

For each question, choose the correct answer.

The young people below are all at a summer camp.
On the opposite page there are descriptions of eight summer camp entertainment activities.
Decide which activity would be the most suitable for the people below.

6 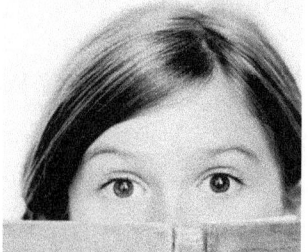 Marta is 14 and enjoys reading. She spends a lot of her free time reading books of all kinds. She'd like to be a writer herself one day. Marta doesn't really enjoy sport. ....

7  Alex is very sporty and competitive and enjoys games of all sorts. He's sociable and has already made lots of friends at summer camp. He has lots of energy and doesn't like sitting still for too long. Alex is 12 years old. ....

8  Elisa is nine and this is her first time at summer camp. Her hobbies are keeping fit and music. She can be a little shy, so she needs to do something that will make her laugh and help her to join in with other children. ....

9  Luke is 13. He is quite a serious, quiet boy and he doesn't really like sports. However, he enjoys chess and other individual games. He also likes music and would like to learn to do more with his musical skills. He plays the piano and the guitar very well. ....

10  Joey is 11. He has a BMX bike but isn't really interested in riding it now. What Joey enjoys more than anything is making things, and he loves doing experiments. Joey likes school but sometimes finds lessons boring. ....

Summer camp entertainment

A **Extreme Board Games**
- Indoors or outdoors
- Lifesize human board games
- Builds teamwork and confidenc

The camp is divided into three teams: red, blue and yellow. Each square on the board represents a different fun activit. One team rolls a giant dice and lands on an activity. Then all three teams compete to win it. Activities include puzzles, games, sports, singing and dancing.
Ages 10–16

B **Laugh-a-Lot Poems**
Toni Evans is a famous poet and author who teaches and inspires young people. Toni shows kids of all ages the fun side of poetry and performs her amusing poems, with lots of opportunities for campers to take part! Toni helps young people to:
- explore their creativity.
- use their imagination.
- discover new ways to communicate their ideas and feelings.

By the end of the show, kids are ready to write their own poetry. Ages 9–16

C **Magic Fun**
Magic for fun has comedy, magic, puppets and lots of opportunity for kids to join in. An energetic and very entertaining show for all ages.
(Headteacher, Avon School)
Our students and staff loved the show and the entire audience laughed from the start. It was interactive and extremely funny.
(Year Leader, Bishop Academy)
Ages 10–16

D **Music Tek**
Brad Simon is a composer, sound designer and producer. He also plays several instruments and sings. Brad shows campers how to use the technology on their phones to create music and sounds for movies and video games. At the end of the show, participants will create an original song.
Ages 10+

E **3-day dance workshop**
You will experience a range of dance styles, including hip hop, street dance and musical theatre. Learn a dance routine, increase your confidence and fitness, AND make new friends.
There will be a filmed performance on the last day of camp.
No previous experience needed
Ages 10–16

F **Crazy Science**
Professor Nuts helps campers learn about science in a simple, fun and entertaining way. There are lots of magic tricks and jokes that help campers understand basic science, maths, machines, chemicals and more. The crazy science show is full of fun, and it's educational too! Kids learn without realising it! It's one of the best ways to help young people learn about scientific methods and take part in practical experiments. Ages 8–12

G **Fitness 4 U:** A great combination of fun and education! The workshop uses magic, comedy and music to get kids excited about healthy eating and exercise! Kids learn our bodies need:
- the right kind of food to stay healthy and moving.
- activities such as biking, swimming and sport.
- creativity – try new and different things to eat, new ways to move and be active. Ages 6+

H **BMX show**
A really exciting show!
See bikes fly through the air and watch riders perform amazing tricks. Lots of opportunities for kids to participate! The show also includes important messages about road safety, doing your best and healthy living.
This amazing outdoor show is great for summer camps, festivals and end-of-term events. All ages

Turn over ▶

Part 3

Questions 11 – 15

For each question, choose the correct answer.

Painting a picture

16-year-old Sonja King writes about her hobby, painting.

I have always enjoyed drawing and painting ever since I can remember. When I was about five, my aunt gave me a beautiful box of coloured paints. I loved all the different colours, but didn't really like just painting the drawings in a child's painting book. I soon realised I preferred drawing my own pictures and colouring them.

Later, I joined my school's art club and one of my paintings was in the summer exhibition. The exhibition was very successful, and I was pleased for the club, but I didn't win a prize. I took too long to decide what I wanted to paint, and then I rushed the actual painting. I was disappointed and angry because I knew I could have done better. However, I learned that in art, it's never a good idea to leave things till the last minute.

After that, I decided to listen to my art teacher more carefully because she had lots of advice. For example, she told me that it wasn't productive to keep restarting work. Most drawings and paintings can be worked on and improved. In fact, they give the finished artwork a richer and more interesting result.

I enjoy painting because you can express yourself and communicate your ideas to others. I love watercolour paints, but also enjoy working with pen and ink. Right now, I'm working on a self-portrait. A lot of artists do self-portraits, so it's a challenge to be creative and paint myself in a unique way. I start by studying photos of myself very carefully. But when I am actually drawing and painting the portrait, I also keep checking in a mirror. That's because it's better to work from 'real life' if possible.

My teacher expects me to practise my drawing skills and brush techniques to make sure my pictures look more realistic. I'm getting good results, and now my self-portrait looks a lot more like me! I'm beginning to realise that, with hard work, there's a chance that I could be a successful artist one day!

Test 7

11 When Sonja was a child, she

- A started drawing when she was five.
- B didn't like painting.
- C drew pictures in a book.
- D enjoyed drawing and painting her own pictures.

12 How did Sonja feel about her painting for the summer exhibition?

- A She took too long to make up her mind about what to paint.
- B She was pleased with it.
- C She was angry with the exhibition judges.
- D She took too long to decide which painting to enter.

13 What advice does Sonja try to follow when she is painting?

- A It's important to make your paintings richer.
- B If your painting isn't very good, then start again.
- C Don't give up on a piece of work too soon.
- D Don't keep thinking about your mistakes.

14 What does Sonja say about her paintings?

- A It's too difficult to do a self-portrait with pen and ink.
- B She only likes working with watercolour paints.
- C She does her paintings from photographs.
- D The best way to do a self-portrait is with a mirror.

15 What might an art expert write about Sonja now?

A
Sonja needs to believe in her own abilities and stop depending on other artists for ideas.

B
Sonja has really improved since her first exhibition and discovered that art is about developing your own style.

C
Sonja seemed disappointed with her last painting, so maybe she should think about working with different materials.

D
Sonja could be a great artist, but she needs to find a teacher to help her develop her painting techniques.

Turn over ▶

Part 4

Questions 16 – 20

Five sentences have been removed from the text below.
For each question, choose the correct answer.
There are three extra sentences which you do not need to use.

Making our park beautiful
by Ben Chilwell, aged 13

Earlier this year, my friends and I went jogging in our local park. There's a special track for joggers and it goes through the woods and past a beautiful lake. [16]   It was spring and there were a lot of flowers and new leaves on the trees, so the park should have been beautiful, but unfortunately it wasn't.

As we jogged around the park, we noticed lots of rubbish everywhere. As well as cigarette ends, there were lots of plastic bottles and paper. [17]   One of my friends picked a broken bottle off the jogging track. That could have been really dangerous!

At the weekend, we all met to organise a rubbish collecting day at the park. My dad pointed out that we needed to be safe and suggested we should get a special tool for collecting litter. [18]   We also bought bags in two colours to put the litter in. [19]

On the day, we collected 14 bags of rubbish from around the lake. To our surprise, a journalist from the local newspaper arrived. [20]   Our group is now much bigger, and we clean the park twice a month. We've noticed that people are now prouder of their park and, as a result, are more careful about their rubbish. That's a good result!

A	Green for things that can be recycled, and black for things that can't.
B	The rubbish bins at the park are emptied twice a week.
C	There was a great photo of us all in the paper that week.
D	There were quite a lot of empty soft drink cans too.
E	There was a football field in the middle of the park
F	We found these online and ordered one each.
G	We put notices up around the school.
H	You can often see ducks on it and sometimes even a swan or two!

Turn over ▶

Part 5

Questions 21 – 26

For each question, choose the correct answer.

Sharks!

Sharks have **(21)** .... for 400 million years. That's even longer than the dinosaurs. There are more than 1,000 species of shark, and new ones are discovered every year. They can weigh **(22)** .... 10,000 kilos and they can be between 20 centimetres and over 12 metres long.

Overfishing and lack of controls are the main reasons for the lower number of sharks we have now. In addition, sharks take a long time to become adults and don't produce many babies. As a **(23)** .... , 30% of shark species could soon die out.

Sharks are necessary for a healthy ocean environment and they are important in the **(24)** .... against climate change. For example, they control the numbers of sea creatures, such as turtles, that eat sea grass. Sea grass **(25)** .... carbon dioxide (an essential gas) from the atmosphere 35 times faster than rainforest trees, so it's important that the grass survives in the ocean and isn't eaten.

Everyone must do everything they can to **(26)** .... these amazing creatures and repair the connection between them and humans.

21 A happened   B existed   C lasted   D been
22 A round   B closely   C near   D nearly
23 A result   B product   C decision   D rule
24 A job   B argument   C fight   D disagreement
25 A keeps   B collects   C puts   D avoids
26 A possess   B have   C hold   D save

Part 6

Questions 27 – 32

For each question, write the correct answer.
Write **one** word for each gap.

Are you a great writer?

Do you like writing? If you do, this short story competition is **(27)** .... you!

The competition aims to encourage young writers **(28)** .... 18 years old. It is open to anyone in the world, but the story must be written in English. We are looking for writing **(29)** .... shows creativity, imagination and a good use of language.

You can write in any style, but it must be your own original work. Your entry can be about any topic, but you should not write more **(30)** .... 500 words.

The winner will receive a prize of £300, and their work will be published in our e-magazine. **(31)** .... addition, two finalists will receive £100 each, and their stories will also appear in our e-magazine.

You cannot enter your story **(32)** .... it has previously appeared on a website or in a book or magazine.

Visit our website to find out more about where to send your entry.

Cambridge B1 Preliminary

Reading

Test 8

© 2025 Prosperity Education.
'Cambridge B1 Preliminary' and 'PET' are brands belonging to The Chancellor, Masters and Scholars of the University of Cambridge and are not associated with Prosperity Education or its products.

Part 1

Questions 1 – 5

For each question, choose the correct answer.

1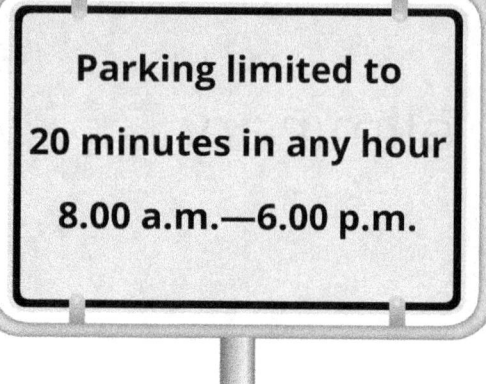

A   You can park at 7.00 p.m. but you can't stay more than 20 minutes.

B   You mustn't park here at 8.30 a.m.

C   You can park for no more than 20 minutes at 3.00 p.m.

2

Football Under-16s Team away match on Saturday. Forms signed by a parent must be handed in at the school office by Thursday lunchtime at the latest or you will lose your place.

A   Those who don't hand in their form on time won't be able to play on Saturday.

B   There are very few places left in the football team.

C   This is the last chance for students to play football in the away match.

3

Dance Workshop

Meeting for anyone interested in joining the workshop on Saturday
Room: D3
Time: 2.30 tomorrow

Previous experience of dance useful, but not essential.

A   You need to be a good dancer in order to join the workshop.

B   All interested students can go to a meeting about the dance workshop.

C   You need to decide before 2.30 tomorrow if you're interested in the dance workshop.

4

School Play
Assistants to help with actors' clothes and make-up urgently required by director.

Training will be given if needed.

A   It is essential to have more make-up assistants, even if they haven't done this before.

B   All assistants will receive training before helping the actors.

C   It is necessary to find a new director to train the assistants.

5

Art Class on Monday

Please remember to bring some nature items (leaves, flowers, etc.) to the lesson. You will need them to create a piece of art on the topic of autumn.

A   Students must collect flowers for a nature project.

B   Students should bring a painting of autumn leaves to the lesson.

C   Students need leaves and flowers to use for a painting or drawing.

Turn over ▶

Part 2

Questions 6 – 10

For each question, choose the correct answer.

The young people and their families below all want to visit the UK during the holidays.
On the opposite page there are descriptions of eight holidays.
Decide which holiday would be the most suitable for the families below.

6  Cora is nine. She loves swimming, especially in the sea. Her mother likes swimming in a pool, but also enjoys beauty treatments when she is on holiday. Cora doesn't like sleeping in tents or in her own room when she is in a hotel.

7  Matt wants to visit the UK to improve his English but also wants to have fun! Matt's family are really interested in British culture. They hope they can combine something useful for Matt with visits to old houses, castles and so on.

8  Emma's family is very sporty and prefers active holidays. Last year they went horse-riding in France. However, this year they want to go to the UK and do a different activity. None of them like walking. Emma is 14 and has two younger brothers.

9  Jessie is 11. She speaks English well, as her father is English. He grew up in Bath and wants to show his daughter the city. Jessie likes the idea but has said she wants to have fun, too. Jessie loves music and would like to see some live music during the holiday.

10  Marco is 12. He's from a musical family who all love classical music and opera. The family don't want to spend the whole holiday in one place. They would like to see several different places during their ten days in the UK. Marco's parents have driven in the UK but didn't enjoy it.

UK holidays

A Mountain bike holiday
Rivers! Forests! Wildlife!
Our off-road holiday offers you th chance to enjoy the English countryside. Accommodation is in our holiday village in the New Forest, with log cabins for up to six people. The hire of mountain bikes is included in the price. Safe off road paths and tracks suitable for all ages and abilities.

B Learn English in England
Improve your English and make friends this summer!
Two-, three- or four-week summer courses in English for under-16s. Fun English lessons in the morning and a variety of historical sightseeing activities in the afternoon. Stay with a friendly and welcoming British family near the school.

C Cool Camping
Great walks! Amazing views! Stay in one of our caravans or tents with incredible views over the Lake District. Wonderful beaches, mountain walks and climbing nearby. We provide:
- Fully equipped tents or caravans
- Shower block and toilets
- Kitchen with kettle
- Accommodation for 2–6 people

Only 20 minutes' walk to beautiful local village with traditional café.

D Bath World Heritage City
This summer why not visit the beautiful, historical city of Bath? Here are just some of the reasons for visiting:
- 2,000-year-old Roman baths and buildings
- 18th-century architecture
- Wonderful art galleries
- Great restaurants, cafés, pubs
- Music events and festivals
- Theatre and street theatre
- Shopping and boutiques

E Beach holiday
The UK has an amazing coast with lots of beaches to explore. Our luxury hotel with spa and indoor swimming pool is located right on the beach in Cornwall. Water sports available, including windsurfing, surfing – and of course, swimming! Go for incredible walks along the beach and coast, or relax on a sun lounger. Family rooms available.

F Camp Best-of-All
The family music festival that really is the best of all, just 10 miles from beautiful Bath. Live bands and artists from the 70s, 80s, 90s and today! For children and adults of all ages, with theatre, art, comedy and poetry, as well as music. Special events for children, such as learning circus skills, or organised games in the Magic Garden. Stay in a luxury tent or campervan. Four days in August.

G Tour Scotland by train
Thinking of coming to the UK this summer for a touring holiday? Don't want to be stuck in traffic jams on long journeys on boring motorways? Worried about driving on the 'wrong side' of the road in an unfamiliar hire car? We've got the answer for you. Tour the beautiful country of Scotland by train. We pick you up at Edinburgh or Glasgow airport and take you straight to your hotel for the first night. The next morning, you're off! Choose from one- or two-week tours.

H Cruise around Britain
The British Isles offers beautiful scenery, miles and miles of countryside, ancient historical sites, cities full of culture and much more. Sail from the south of the country with its golden beaches, past the island of Ireland and up to the mountain landscape of Scotland. Stop in seven places to see the sights during our 15-day cruise.
All food and drinks are included in the low, low price!
Cabins for one, two or four people.

Turn over ▶

Part 3

Questions 11 – 15

For each question, choose the correct answer.

Play to win

16-year-old Isabella Jones writes about her hobby, badminton.

I think I got my love of badminton from my mother. She was good at the sport and used to play every weekend. My father and I often used to go and watch her games. According to my father, I sometimes got so excited that I shouted and clapped when Mum scored a point. I was only about four at the time, so I don't remember that very well.

However, not long after that, my mother started to teach me how to play tennis and badminton. I don't think she was expecting me to be very good at the games, but she said sport was a great way to exercise. I didn't enjoy tennis, but I really loved badminton. Eventually, we stopped the tennis completely and just concentrated on badminton. I played the game whenever I could, and I tried hard to get better at it. And, with Mum's help, I did! By the time I was nine, I was a member of the school team, and I played in school matches every weekend.

Everyone said what a good player I was, but none of my school friends ever wanted to play doubles with me, and I didn't understand why. In doubles matches, I got most of the points. I thought that was a good thing, and I thought everyone would want to be my partner – but they didn't.

In the end, I spoke to my sports teacher, Miss Hammond, about the problem. I asked her why the others didn't want to be my doubles partner. Her reply confused me even more. She said, 'Because you score almost all the points.' Then she went on to explain. 'Doubles is a game where both players in the team work together. When people play with you, they don't get a chance to play at all, because you go for every shot.' Suddenly I began to understand. I was giving my partners the message that I was a better player and I didn't need them.

Since then, I have played doubles differently and thought about my partners a lot more. My new method has worked. Now there is a list of people who want to be my partner ... and we still win all our games!

11 Isabella

   A   watched her parents play badminton when she was four.
   B   started to play badminton when she was four.
   C   remembers shouting at her mother's badminton games when she was four.
   D   frequently went to watch her mother play badminton.

12 Why did Isabella's mother start to teach her badminton?

   A   She wanted her daughter to be a good player.
   B   She wanted Isabella to get some exercise.
   C   She was a badminton teacher.
   D   She wanted Isabella to be good at the game so that they could play together.

13 What was the problem in the school team?

   A   Isabella didn't want to play doubles.
   B   Too many people wanted to be Isabella's partner in doubles.
   C   Nobody in the team wanted to play doubles with Isabella.
   D   Isabella didn't score points in doubles matches.

14 What did Miss Hammond help Isabella to understand?

   A   Both players are equally important in a doubles team.
   B   Isabella should continue to play all her games in the same way.
   C   She was a good player because she scored the most points.
   D   She was a better player than most of her teammates.

15 What might a sports journalist write about Isabella now?

A
| Isabella needs to believe in her own abilities and stop depending on good luck when she plays. |

B
| Isabella is a great player and has improved since she discovered that doubles is a team game even though there is only one other person. |

C
| Isabella didn't score as many points in her last match, so maybe she should watch the shuttlecock more closely. |

D
| Isabella could be a great player, but she needs to work on improving her game. |

Turn over ▶

Part 4

Questions 16 – 20

Five sentences have been removed from the text below.
For each question, choose the correct answer.
There are three extra sentences which you do not need to use.

Modern marketing
by Joel Smith, aged 15

I'm interested in doing a business degree, so last week I went to a talk about marketing. I learned lots of things that I didn't really know before, especially about digital marketing. For example, did you know that a digital ad which includes a video gets over 90% more views? **16** ____ So, that's a huge challenge for people in digital marketing.

What else did I learn? Well, firstl , marketing is not the same as advertising. Adverts are a part of marketing, but in fact it's much more than that. Marketing is a method for getting as many customers as possible. **17** ____ Most importantly, in marketing you identify people's needs and then try to satisfy those needs.

Marketing to young people of our age needs to be different. **18** ____ Young people want to know what experience or feeling the product will give them, and how it will benefit them. **19** ____ Marketing to this group of consumers needs to use lots of videos and posts on social media.

Finally, young people are a huge, important market and will often persuade their parents to buy some everyday products they've seen advertised. **20** ____ However, some companies see this as a bad thing, so they refuse to market to children.

A	But your average customer only watches a video for about eight seconds before clicking onto something different
B	Children are not able to understand the difference between good and bad adverts
C	Examples of such products include breakfast cereals or fast-food meals.
D	Customers are buying more and more products online.
E	Or, to put it another way, it connects producers with customers.
F	That is more interesting than the features of the product itself.
G	TV advertising today is much cheaper than 10 years ago.
H	We don't respond very well to traditional adverts and marketing.

Turn over ▶

Part 5

Questions 21 – 26

For each question, choose the correct answer.

Amazing eyes

In your head, you have a pair of cameras that are at work from the moment you wake up **(21)** .... you go to sleep at night. Your eyes are only 2.5cm wide, but with them you can see a tiny ant on the **(22)** .... or a bird high in the air. They can operate in bright sunlight or at night, and take in information about the world around you, including shapes, colours and movement. You actually see things the wrong **(23)** .... up, so your brain has to turn the images the right way up.

Your body has several ways to **(24)** .... your eyes, because your sight is very important. One way is opening and closing your eyes, known as blinking. We do this **(25)** .... while we are awake, in fact, more than 10,000 times a day! Every blink washes away bacteria and spreads a fluid over your eyes to prevent them becoming too dry. If anything gets too close, your eyes **(26)**..................... by closing in milliseconds.

21	A while	B unless	C until	D to
22	A land	B ground	C garden	D flower
23	A way	B method	C view	D look
24	A treat	B prevent	C protect	D save
25	A usually	B repeatedly	C again	D frequent
26	A answer	B reply	C act	D respond

Part 6

Questions 27 – 32

For each question, write the correct answer.
Write **one** word for each gap.

Computer health
by Liz Potter

Our grandparents did not have computers **(27)** .... they were young. If they wanted to find something out, they had to visit a library. For entertainment and socialising, they **(28)** .... to go out and meet friends or play sports.

Today we use computers for all those things ... and a lot more. However, the latest research shows **(29)** .... computers are not always good for our health. In some cases, long periods at the computer can lead to physical problems **(30)** .... your body and your eyes. Some children lose some of their social skills and **(31)** .... ability to be creative, too. Children sometimes visit dangerous websites by accident. Our grandparents did not have these problems.

To stay healthy, make sure you sit in a comfortable position at the computer and have regular breaks. Look away from the screen every twenty minutes or so, and go outside for a walk occasionally. Most important of all, stay **(32)** .... from unsafe websites.

Cambridge B1 Preliminary

Reading

Test 9

Part 1

Questions 1 – 5

For each question, choose the correct answer.

1

Swimming Pool

No children under 12 allowed in pool unless accompanied by an adult.

A   Children younger than twelve are not allowed in the pool.

B   Children of 11 and younger can only swim if they are with someone over 18.

C   Only adults are allowed to swim here.

2

To: Students interested in exchange visits

All forms must be signed and handed in to the school office by 9.00 a.m. on Friday, November 1st.
No forms will be accepted after this date.

A   Those who don't provide forms on time won't be able to do the student exchange.

B   There are very few places left for the student exchange.

C   Forms for students interested in exchange visits will be handed out on Friday.

3

School public speaking competition

Anyone interested in taking part, please sign below.

NOTE: You are permitted to enter no more than two groups.

A   You must have signed permission to take part in the public speaking competition.

B   You have to limit the number of public speaking groups you take part in.

C   You need to write your name here to get more information about the competition.

4

Work Experience

Local nursery school urgently requires assistants for work experience. Previous experience with young children (1–4 years) welcome but not essential, as training will be given.

Contact Mrs Dunn for more information.

A It is necessary for Mrs Dunn to employ only trained assistants.

B It is important for all assistants to have training before applying.

C The nursery school needs more assistants, even if they haven't worked with children before.

5

SCIENCE MUSEUM VISIT

Please remember to bring a packed lunch with you as the museum café will be closed. No drinks in cans, please!

A Students should check the opening hours of the café.

B Students won't get lunch unless they take food with them.

C Students can take anything they like for lunch.

Turn over ▶

Part 2

Questions 6 – 10

For each question, choose the correct answer.

The young people below all want to visit a large mall at the weekend.
On the opposite page there are descriptions of eight stores.
Decide which store would be the most suitable for the people below.

6  Betty loves shopping in malls! She needs to buy a birthday present for her best friend, Grace. Grace likes reading, table tennis and fashion. Betty has about £5 to spend.

7  Mario doesn't really like shopping, but he needs to buy a leaving present for his English teacher. He and his friends have collected £20. They bought the teacher some bath products for her birthday, so Mario wants to get something different, and special.

8  Elena is going on holiday to the Caribbean with her parents. She needs some clothes for a warm climate, including a new swimming costume. She has quite a long list of things to buy, so she has to shop carefully.

9  Harry is very sporty, so his sports shoes never last long. He needs some new ones now, but he can't afford expensive designer shoes. When his friends show him their trendy trainers, he always says, 'Mine are for playing sport in, not for hanging out.'

10  Jack needs to buy a present for his brother, Lucas, who's only four. He really has no idea what to get him, although his mother says Lucas loves books. Jack also knows Lucas likes painting and drawing.

West shopping mall

A   Modern Look
Visit us for cool fashion!
Great prices and sizes (6–20).
Latest winter clothes now in stock.
Visit our men's department for suits and work clothes.
SPECIAL! We still have some summer items, including beachwear – discounts of up to 50%.

B   Top Trainers
THE shoe store in West Mall!
All the top names in sports shoes.
Choose from thousands of styles, including footwear using the latest technology. All sizes available for men, women and kids.
Top Trainers offers cool, stylish choices!

C   Additions
A one-stop shop for stylish accessories: bags, belts, scarves, jewellery and much more.
Great prices, from only £2.00!
Home to the latest fashion trends for today's woman.
Our store in West Mall has recently had a makeover. Why not call in and explore?

D   Discount Sports Store
Stylish sportswear at a price you can afford. Get everything you need for all the sports you play – and pay half the price of the 'big name' stores. All colours and sizes for men and women, boys and girls.

E   Choc-o-love
Luxury chocolates that are exciting and beautiful.

Gifts	Eco
Choose your chocolates and we will put them in an attractive gift box. Prices from £5.00.	Everything made from organic products on our own farm in the Caribbean. Our workers are paid a fair wage. Gift boxes and bags 100% recyclable.

F   Bubbles
Our luxury soaps, hair and skincare products will delight your senses: sight, smell and touch! Everything is handmade from fresh fruit and vegetables. We only use the finest oils, flowers, herbs and plants. NO plastic. NEVER tested on animals. Visit us for great gifts or to spoil yourself!

G   Books! Books! Books!
We sell ... books ... and nothing else.
- fiction & non-fiction
- colouring books
- picture books
- puzzle books
- large-print books
- e-readers with e-books already loaded

Books for all ages and interests.
Visit **Books! Books! Books!** for ... books!

H   Toys 4 All
Opening SOON in West Mall!
We will have something for every child, from new-born to 12.

Toys	Board Games
Puzzles	Computer Games
Books	Music

Everything you need for your child ... or for adults who want to have fun!

Turn over ▶

Part 3

Questions 11 – 15

For each question, choose the correct answer.

My musical family

15-year-old Olivia Moss writes about her hobby, music.

My family is very musical. My four brothers and sisters and I all play at least one instrument, including the piano, violin, cello and flute. I wanted to learn the double bass, too, which is a stringed instrument as big as me, but my parents said they wouldn't be able to get it in our minibus!

When we were younger, my parents spent all their time taking us to various music lessons and concerts. But it was worth it, because my older brother and sister got accepted into a famous national music academy. I hope to go there, too, so I'm practising two pieces for an audition for their summer school. If you get to the summer school, you have a better chance of a place at the main academy.

My parents are amazing, and it has been very expensive for them to support our dreams. It has also taken a lot of their time and hard work. Sometimes we had to travel a very long way. They could only afford an old minibus to transport all of us plus our instruments. Once it broke down on the way to a concert, so we had to travel the rest of the way in three separate taxis!

When I was about 12, I entered a local music competition and played a piano piece. I chose it because I thought it would show what a good piano technique I had. I was disappointed because I came second. I played well and got high marks, but the judges said that I didn't put enough feeling into the music. That was quite hard to take.

Our family is now quite famous. Our music group won a TV talent competition and my sister played at a wedding for a celebrity couple. We have just finished making our first album That was great because we all practised together, whereas usually we all go off to different concert and events. We actually learned a lot from each other. But my mum says she likes it best when we just play freely at home simply because we love it.

11 In Olivia's family

    A   the children each play four instruments.
    B   there are nine children.
    C   there are five children
    D   one of her brothers or sisters plays the double bass.

12 Why does Olivia want to go to the music academy summer school?

    A   because she may then be more likely to get into the main academy
    B   because her brother and sister are going
    C   because her parents don't want to drive her to music lessons in the summer
    D   because she's learned two pieces of music

13 Why does Olivia think her parents are amazing?

    A   They paid for taxis to concerts.
    B   It took a lot of effort, time and money for the family s musical education.
    C   They bought an old minibus, so they had more money to pay for lessons.
    D   It was very difficult to transport all the children and all their instrument

14 What does Olivia say about the music competition?

    A   She played well but didn't get very good marks.
    B   She didn't like the piece of music she chose.
    C   The judges made a poor decision.
    D   She found it difficult to deal with the judges' decision.

15 What might a music journalist write about Olivia now?

A
Olivia needs to believe in her own abilities and stop depending on her brothers and sisters when they play together.

B
Olivia has really grown up since making an album with her family, and discovered that you must enjoy the music to be a great musician.

C
Olivia looked exhausted when she finished her last piano competition, so maybe she should think about playing less difficult music

D
Olivia could be a great musician, but she needs to find a teacher to take her all the way to the big competitions.

Turn over ▶

Part 4

Questions 16 – 20

Five sentences have been removed from the text below.
For each question, choose the correct answer.
There are three extra sentences which you do not need to use.

Smart eating!
by Ellie Dane, aged 13

I love cooking and I'd like a career in food at some time in the future. I really enjoy watching cookery programmes, and recently I watched one about how to eat well. [16] I learned that good food is important to prevent illnesses and to keep your hair, skin and nails looking great.

As a young child, the first things I learned to cook were cakes and biscuits. [17] But of course, these things are not all that good for you if you eat them every day, because they contain too much sugar. Sugar is extremely bad for you, partly because too much can lead to an illness called diabetes. [18]

So, instead of cakes and biscuits, I try to prepare 'smart food' now, with lots of vegetables, and sometimes fish or chicken. People often think healthy food means salad, but there are lots of other possibilities. [19] It isn't too spicy, and I put yoghurt in it as well as lots of vegetables. It's really tasty and delicious. [20] I have also learned that it's much healthier if you replace white rice with brown in these dishes. Of course, I still have a piece of cake occasionally. I'm not perfect! But not every day, like before.

A	And, of course, it can cause lots of problems with your teeth.
B	Avoid eating red meat as much as possible.
C	Fast food and takeaways are bad for your health, too.
D	I also do a vegetarian version with nuts, which is low in fat and very healthy.
E	I didn't realise, until I saw this programme, how important healthy eating really is.
F	It was fun to make them and then decorate them with sweets and chocolate.
G	It's really important to eat breakfast every day.
H	For example, my favourite recipe is one for chicken curry.

Part 5

Questions 21 – 26

For each question, choose the correct answer.

Plastic!

What do you think of when you think about plastic? Most people would **(21)** .... think of plastic bags to carry shopping, and boxes to keep food fresh. And it's true that huge **(22)** .... of plastic are used for packing and wrapping. But it can also be used, for example, in a jumper or in a pair of gloves.

A useful feature of plastic is that it can be made into any **(23)** .... We use it in place of many other materials, including glass, wood and metal, and we decorate and build things with it.

Some **(24)** .... forms of plastic were made from parts of animals and plants. Later, plastic played an essential part in the development of cars, in film for the movie industry and in **(25)** .... electricity to homes and industry.

A huge advantage of plastic is that it can be very strong and **(26)** .... a long time. That is also a disadvantage, because plastic rubbish stays in the ground or in the oceans for thousands of years.

21	A	immediately	B	quickly	C	later	D	suddenly
22	A	sums	B	amounts	C	lots	D	numbers
23	A	sort	B	figure	C	structure	D	shape
24	A	beginning	B	early	C	starting	D	firstly
25	A	moving	B	having	C	bringing	D	collecting
26	A	lasts	B	lives	C	continues	D	stays

Part 6

Questions 27 – 32

For each question, write the correct answer.

Learning English in England
by Dani Alves

Have you thought about learning English in England and staying **(27)** .... an English family in your summer holidays?

I stayed in a town called Bournemouth, **(28)** .... is on the south coast. It's famous for its beautiful long sandy beach.

At the school, we had lessons in the mornings. There were seven different nationalities in my class, **(29)** .... we had to speak English all the time. **(30)** .... we did some grammar, we also had lots of songs and games, so we never got bored. In the afternoons, we did activities and sports.

I also learned a lot of English outside class, with my family. At mealtimes, I had to speak English because the family didn't speak any Spanish. My family was very kind and friendly, and I made good friends with their son, Jordan, **(31)** .... is about the same age as me. I enjoyed it **(32)** .... much that I hope to return next year!

Cambridge B1 Preliminary

Reading

Test 10

Part 1

Questions 1 – 5

For each question, choose the correct answer.

1

Lake Farm Campsite

No dogs, unless booked in advance. Maximum two dogs per tent.

A   All campers must reserve a place in advance.

B   Campers with dogs are not allowed on this site.

C   Campers bringing a dog should contact the campsite before arriving.

2

To: School magazine contributors

All articles for the school magazine must be given to the editor by Tuesday lunchtime at the latest or your article will not be included.

A   There is not enough space for everyone's article to be included.

B   Those who don't hand in their article on time won't be part of the magazine.

C   This is the last chance for students to join the magazine team.

3

Special offer: 20% discount with your first order!

Only one discount permitted per home address.

To receive your discount, enter your details below.

A   You need to write your name and address to get more information.

B   Your family can also receive special offers from this company.

C   You must provide information to get money off when you place an order.

4

Beach Clean

Helpers urgently required for beach clean-up this Saturday.

If possible, please bring a large black bin bag with you.

Students under 16 welcome, but you need your parents' permission.

A   It is essential to have more helpers, even if they are not yet 16.

B   It is important that parents allow their children to take part in the beach clean.

C   The beach clean cannot take place if there aren't enough bin bags.

5

Cookery Class on Monday

Remember to bring the ingredients below to the lesson — you will need them to make biscuits! I will give you the full recipe on Monday.

Ingredients: flour, butter, sugar, milk, 2 eggs, chocolate

A   Students should check that they have all the instructions for making biscuits.

B   Students need to bring certain food items for the cookery lesson.

C   Students must write a recipe using the ingredients in the list.

Turn over ▶

Part 2

Questions 6 – 10

For each question, choose the correct answer.

The young people below all want to go to the capital for the day.
On the opposite page there are descriptions of things they could do in the capital.
Decide which activity would be the most suitable for the people below.

6  Ethan wants to do something which involves water. He loves swimming, fishing or just travelling by boat. He has a tank in his bedroom with brightly coloured fish, and there are huge orange fish from some far-off place in his parents' pond. ....

7  Elsa wants to study biology at university. She is a keen gardener and is particularly interested in unusual flowers. She's not interested in architecture and doesn't want to waste the day going round shops. ....

8  Sophie wants to see as much of the city as possible, but she doesn't want to go up any tall buildings, because heights make her feel sick. She sometimes feels ill on boats, too. ....

9  Tom loves history and wants to go to the capital because he knows that many of the buildings there are extremely old. His mother can't walk very well, though, so they will have to plan the day carefully. Tom has heard that the best views of the city are from the river. ....

10  Nick is travelling with his family, including his grandparents, so they need to find something which is good for everyone. Nick would love to go on safari one day to see the famous animals of Africa. His sister is a birdwatcher, and his little brother has a pet spider. ....

A day out in the capital

A Manor Gardens
In our huge glass houses, we have some of the strangest and most beautiful plants in the world. The original owner of Manor Gardens travelled the world and brought back many of the trees and flowers herself in the 19th century. Since then, other biologists have contributed to the collection, making it possibly the best in the world. If the weather is fine, why not have a picnic in the grounds?

B River Cruise
Take a one-way or return cruise from West Station to Capital Bridge (or the other way round) and see the sights of the capital from the river.
Listen to an audio commentary as you cruise past all the great buildings of the capital, including the centre of government and the royal palace.
Food and drinks available on the boat.

C Water World
In the heart of the city, you can see wonderful ocean and sea creatures, from sharks and clownfish to jellyfish and seahorses. Walk under the sea in our amazing glass tunnels. Swim with the dolphins (at 3.00 and 4.00 each day).

D The Open Bus Tour
Travel all around the city on one of our two routes:
Blue route: Shopping
Green route: Famous buildings
On each route, you can get on or off at any of the 15 stops. Buses run every 15 minutes in summer. Audio commentary available.

E The Great Wheel
The newest attraction in the capital! Get on our wheel and ride high into the air, then look out over the whole of the city.
Travel with your family in your own cabin, or mix with other people.
Have tea and cakes in your cabin as you travel round. (Trip takes 30 minutes.)

F The Capital by Night
Why not end the day with a bus tour around the capital by night? See all the lights and magnificent buildings of the capital. The tour includes a speedy ride in a glass lift to the top of the highest building in the capital, from where you get fantastic views across the city. The tour starts at sunset each day and lasts one hour.

G Capital Zoo
This is one of the best zoos in the world, with something for everyone. We have animals from every part of the world, including lions, tigers and elephants.
We also have some of the smallest animals in our insect house, and a wonderful selection of birds, like parrots and flamingos, in Bird World. Special low price for large groups.

H Elver Castle
Just three miles from the centre of the capital is one of the oldest castles in the country. A building has been on this site for at least 1,000 years.
Explore hundreds of rooms full of historical items from over the centuries. Climb to the top of the Great Tower and look out across the capital.
Note: Many steps in and around the castle, so not suitable for people with walking difficulties.

Turn over ▶

Part 3

Questions 11 – 15

For each question, choose the correct answer.

Revising for an exam

16-year-old Morgan White writes about the best ways to revise.

When I was younger, we had some important exams at school. I did OK, but I was a bit disappointed with my results. My teacher said I was intelligent, but that I needed to plan my revision better. So I did some research online and found quite a lot of suggestions that I thought were really good. I started to use some of the ideas for my next exams, and my results were much better.

I used to revise a few days before the exam, but now I realise you need to start revision months before. The important thing is to make a revision timetable. You can download one and then fill it in with dates, times and revision topics. However, if you do this, you should make sure you include time to relax and have fun, too! You should probably take a break for a few minutes every 25 to 30 minutes, because you will remember a lot more this way.

A suitable place to study is a good idea. It should have a light and anything you need, such as pens, nearby. Make sure your phone and TV are switched off, so there are no distractions. Be honest with yourself, too. Does playing music really help you to concentrate, or is it another distraction?

Make sure your notes are clear and neat, but they don't need to look beautiful. You can use a variety of techniques with your notes. For example, turn them into flashcards or rewrite your notes from memory. Or you can make quiz questions from your notes and work with a friend or group to answer them.

Everybody is different, but the most useful technique for me was to make a topic into a PowerPoint presentation. The most important advantage of this is you can use the creative side of your brain. It involves lots of skills, including organising information. Writing and typing the information helps you to remember it. Teaching a topic to others is one of the best ways to learn, so if you can actually give the presentation to your study group or class, it's really effective.

11 Morgan

   A failed his exams when he was younger.
   B used the internet to look for revision techniques.
   C got some good advice from his teacher about how to revise.
   D felt that some suggestions for revision were disappointing.

12 What's Morgan's opinion of revision timetables?

   A You need regular breaks of about half an hour.
   B You need to timetable lots of fun.
   C You will remember more if you use a timetable.
   D You shouldn't put too many study times in it.

13 What things can help you to revise?

   A playing music
   B a quiet area with the things you need for studying
   C playing quiz games with your friends
   D copying your friend's notes neatly

14 What does Morgan say about presentations?

   A They have several different benefits for revising.
   B All students will find giving presentations useful.
   C Going to presentations has many advantages.
   D It's important to show your teacher your presentation.

15 What might a teacher write in a report about Morgan now?

A
| Morgan needs to believe in his own abilities and stop depending on good luck when he takes exams. |

B
| Morgan looked exhausted when he arrived for his exam, so he should make sure he gets enough sleep. |

C
| Morgan has really improved his study skills and discovered that exams are a good opportunity to show what you know. |

D
| Morgan could get really good marks, but he needs to do more practice tests before his exams. |

Turn over ▶

Part 4

Questions 16 – 20

Five sentences have been removed from the text below.
For each question, choose the correct answer.
There are three extra sentences which you do not need to use.

How to make decisions
by Maria Richards, aged 17

I'm studying psychology, and last week some of our lessons were about decision-making and why some people find it so difficult **16**____ By the end of the week, we had a much better idea of the reasons why some decisions are difficult. We also learnt about some solutions.

One problem is that sometimes we have too many decisions to make every day. **17**____ Psychologists suggest you reduce the number of basic decisions so that you can use your brain power for more important ones. **18**____

In business, sales assistants know that people are actually more comfortable with fewer choices. **19**____ However, in everyday life we are often faced with too many possible choices for a decision. In this situation, you need to think carefully about each choice, and not accept any that might be a little dangerous or too uncertain.

Another suggestion for improving your decision-making skills is to pretend you are advising a friend. What advice would you give them? Finally, don't spend too long thinking about the decision, especially if other people are waiting for your choice. **20**____ Whatever you do, make sure you go with that decision and don't change your mind later!

A	And they use that information to sell you a product!
B	Everyone in the class found it a fascinating area, and a few students admitted they really didn't like making decisions.
C	Give a logical reason for your decision.
D	If necessary, set a timer.
E	Presidents and prime ministers have important decisions to make every day.
F	Recently, my parents took ages to decide what new car to buy.
G	So, you could make a habit of having the same thing for lunch every day, to avoid making that basic decision each day.
H	Some of these are quite basic, like deciding what to wear or what to have for lunch.

Turn over ▶

Part 5

Questions 21 – 26

For each question, choose the correct answer.

The moon

It's easy to see the moon in the night sky, **(21)** .... it is nearly 400,000 kilometres away. The moon shines with the light of the sun. So, the moon looks different at different time of the month, **(22)** .... on the positions of the moon, the sun and the Earth. However, it always shows us the same side. From Earth, we're unable to see the hidden dark side of the moon.

The moon takes 27.3 days to travel around the Earth. It has a diameter of 3,475 kilometres and is about a quarter of the **(23** ....of our planet.

Recent evidence shows that the moon was formed from a piece of the Earth which **(24)** .... off about 4.4 billion years ago.

The moon has an important **(25)** .... on our planet, and it might be what makes life on Earth possible. The **(26)** .... of the moon affects the rise and fall of the sea, and helps to keep our climate fairly regular.

21	A although	B despite	C even	D however
22	A conditional	B differing	C depending	D dependent
23	A measure	B shape	C amount	D size
24	A broke	B got	C made	D cut
25	A took	B effect	C result	D consequence
26	A weight	B power	C attract	D pull

Part 6

Questions 27 – 32

For each question, write the correct answer.

Online learning
by Josie Truman

Recently, I've had some English lessons online and I was surprised because I enjoyed them more **(27)** .... I thought I would.

I know some students have online lessons **(28)** .... large numbers of students, maybe a hundred! I think it must **(29)** .... quite difficult for the teacher in that situation, because it's harder to get to know your students.

However, in my lessons, there are only **(30)** .... 15 and 20 of us. Our teacher, Anne, is great because she makes the lesson fun and very interactive. I find it really exciting that I **(31)** .... meet students from different countries, all in one online classroom.

We mostly do listening and speaking activities in our lessons, and often watch short videos. The best thing is when Anne allows us to write or draw on the whiteboard. I **(32** .... enjoy seeing everyone's answers or comments in the chat box.

Answers

Practice Test 1: Reading Marking Key

Part 1 5 marks

1. A
2. C
3. B
4. A
5. C

Part 2 5 marks

6. D
7. G
8. B
9. F
10. E

Part 3 5 marks

11. B
12. C
13. A
14. C
15. A

Part 4 5 marks

16. B
17. H
18. A
19. F
20. E

Part 5 6 marks

21. A
22. B
23. A
24. C
25. B
26. A

Part 6 6 marks

27. was
28. had
29. part
30. There
31. Because / As / Since
32. which

Practice Test 2: Reading Marking Key

Part 1 — 5 marks

1. C
2. B
3. A
4. B
5. B

Part 2 — 5 marks

6. E
7. B
8. A
9. G
10. D

Part 3 — 5 marks

11. A
12. C
13. C
14. D
15. C

Part 4 — 5 marks

16. C
17. E
18. G
19. B
20. D

Part 5 — 6 marks

21. A
22. C
23. B
24. D
25. A
26. B

Part 6 — 6 marks

27. If
28. to
29. are
30. was
31. which / that
32. will

Practice Test 3: Reading Marking Key

Part 1 — 5 marks

1. C
2. A
3. B
4. C
5. B

Part 2 — 5 marks

6. A
7. F
8. G
9. C
10. D

Part 3 — 5 marks

11. C
12. A
13. B
14. D
15. C

Part 4 — 5 marks

16. B
17. E
18. G
19. H
20. D

Part 5 — 6 marks

21. C
22. B
23. D
24. C
25. A
26. B

Part 6 — 6 marks

27. with
28. there
29. well
30. what
31. playing / doing / learning / trying
32. if

Practice Test 4: Reading Marking Key

Part 1   5 marks

1 B
2 A
3 A
4 C
5 B

Part 2   5 marks

6   G
7   D
8   E
9   B
10 F

Part 3   5 marks

11 B
12 C
13 D
14 A
15 B

Part 4   5 marks

16 C
17 D
18 A
19 F
20 H

Part 5   6 marks

21 B
22 C
23 D
24 A
25 C
26 B

Part 6   6 marks

27 but
28 do
29 it / that
30 if
31 who / that
32 was

Practice Test 5: Reading Marking Key

Part 1		5 marks
1	A	
2	B	
3	C	
4	B	
5	C	

Part 2		5 marks
6	F	
7	D	
8	C	
9	G	
10	H	

Part 3		5 marks
11	C	
12	A	
13	B	
14	C	
15	C	

Part 4		5 marks
16	F	
17	B	
18	H	
19	E	
20	A	

Part 5		6 marks
21	B	
22	A	
23	D	
24	B	
25	A	
26	C	

Part 6		6 marks
27	If	
28	between / from	
29	which / that	
30	to	
31	need / have	
32	will	

Practice Test 6: Reading Marking Key

Part 1		5 marks
1	A	
2	C	
3	B	
4	C	
5	A	

Part 2		5 marks
6	D	
7	B	
8	H	
9	G	
10	E	

Part 3		5 marks
11	C	
12	A	
13	B	
14	D	
15	B	

Part 4		5 marks
16	D	
17	E	
18	G	
19	B	
20	A	

Part 5		6 marks
21	B	
22	A	
23	D	
24	C	
25	A	
26	D	

Part 6		6 marks
27	an	
28	of	
29	If	
30	after	
31	weather	
32	use	

Practice Test 7: Reading Marking Key

Part 1 5 marks

1. B
2. C
3. A
4. B
5. C

Part 2 5 marks

6. B
7. A
8. C
9. D
10. F

Part 3 5 marks

11. D
12. A
13. C
14. D
15. B

Part 4 5 marks

16. H
17. D
18. F
19. A
20. C

Part 5 6 marks

21. B
22. D
23. A
24. C
25. B
26. D

Part 6 6 marks

27. for
28. under
29. that/which
30. than
31. In
32. if

Practice Test 8: Reading Marking Key

Part 1		5 marks
1	C	
2	A	
3	B	
4	A	
5	C	

Part 2		5 marks
6	E	
7	B	
8	A	
9	F	
10	G	

Part 3		5 marks
11	D	
12	B	
13	C	
14	A	
15	B	

Part 4		5 marks
16	A	
17	E	
18	H	
19	F	
20	C	

Part 5		6 marks
21	C	
22	B	
23	A	
24	C	
25	B	
26	D	

Part 6		6 marks
27	when	
28	had/used	
29	that	
30	with/for	
31	their/the	
32	away	

Practice Test 9: Reading Marking Key

Part 1   5 marks

1. B
2. A
3. B
4. C
5. B

Part 2   5 marks

6. C
7. E
8. A
9. D
10. G

Part 3   5 marks

11. C
12. A
13. B
14. D
15. B

Part 4   5 marks

16. E
17. F
18. A
19. H
20. D

Part 5   6 marks

21. A
22. B
23. D
24. B
25. C
26. A

Part 6   6 marks

27. with
28. which
29. and
30. Although
31. who
32. so

Practice Test 10: Reading Marking Key

Part 1   5 marks

1. C
2. B
3. C
4. A
5. B

Part 2   5 marks

6. C
7. A
8. D
9. B
10. G

Part 3   5 marks

11. B
12. C
13. B
14. A
15. C

Part 4   5 marks

16. B
17. H
18. G
19. A
20. D

Part 5   6 marks

21. A
22. C
23. D
24. A
25. B
26. D

Part 6   6 marks

27. than
28. with/including
29. be
30. between/about/approximately
31. can
32. also

www.ingramcontent.com/pod-product-compliance
Lightning Source LLC
Chambersburg PA
CBHW081103070526
44584CB00021B/3180